FOREX
WAVE THEORY

FOREX
WAVE THEORY

A Technical Analysis for Spot
and Futures Currency Traders

JAMES L. BICKFORD

McGraw-Hill
New York   Chicago   San Francisco
Lisbon   London   Madrid   Mexico City
Milan   New Delhi   San Juan   Seoul
Singapore   Sydney   Toronto

ISBN-13: 978-0-07-149302-4
ISBN-10: 0-07-149302-6

Library of Congress Cataloging-in-Publication Data

Bickford, Jim L.
  Forex wave theory / James L. Bickford.
    p. cm.
  Includes bibliographical references and index.
    ISBN 0-07-149302-6 (hardcover: alk. paper)   1. Foreign exchange market.
2. Speculation.   3. Investment analysis.   I. Title.

HG3851.B47 2007
332.4'5--dc22   2006103347

Contents

List of Figures
and Tables

Part 6. Three-Wave Cycles

Part 7. Four-Wave Cycles

Part 8. Five-Wave Cycles

Acknowledgment

I wish to thank Paul J. Szeligowski, friend and economic analyst, for his editorial assistance in the preparation of this book. His insightful recommendations and novel ideas proved invaluable in researching the nature and occasionally cryptic relationships that arise when scrutinizing financial wave theories.

Introduction

Trading in the foreign exchange currency markets recently has exceeded $2 trillion a day, and this figure is expected to double within the next five years. The reason for this astonishing surge in trading popularity is quite simple: no commissions, low transaction costs, easy access to online currency markets, no middlemen, no fixed-lot order sizes, high liquidity, low margin with high leverage, and limited regulations. These factors already have attracted the attention of both neophyte traders and veteran speculators in other financial markets. Traders who have not yet passed the currency rites of initiation are encouraged to read *Getting Started in Currency Trading*, by Michael Archer and James Bickford (Wiley, 2005).

ABOUT THIS BOOK

The purpose of this book is to provide spot and futures currency traders with an innovative approach to the technical analysis of price fluctuations in the foreign exchange markets. Financial markets move in waves. These waves, in turn, form business cycles that are components of even larger cycles. Knowledge of *why* this phenomenon occurs is not critical (although very absorbing) to technical analysts. This aspect of trading is left to fundamental analysts. Instead, it is the *where* and the *when* questions that are critical to all technical analysts. Determining the direction of subsequent cycles (and component waves) is the paramount goal.

HOW THIS BOOK IS ORGANIZED

There are ten major divisions within this book.

Part 1:   Currency Markets

Much of the material in this section is a quick overview of both spot currency markets and currency futures. This includes definitions for the technical jargon used throughout the remainder of this book.

Part 2:   Technical Analysis

The four most significant categories within technical analysis (i.e., pattern recognition, econometric models, crossover trading systems, and wave theory) are reviewed in the section.

Part 3:   Reversal Charts

The essential reversal charts used by wave theoreticians are explained in detail, with the advantages and disadvantages of each method being highlighted. This section lays down the foundation for the remainder of the book.

Part 4:   Brief History of Wave Theory

Wave theory has a long and intriguing history. All the major systems are scrutinized with close attention to the Elliott wave principle.

Parts 5–9:   Cycles

Different length cycles (two through six waves) are analyzed in detail, with special emphasis on their predictive reliability. Ratio analysis and cycle frequencies play an important role in determining the level of confidence for each forecast.

Part 10:   Advanced Topics

The salient cycle property called *fractality* is examined in detail. This is the characteristic where a single wave may be composed of even smaller waves. In this fashion, forecasts may be calculated at two different fractal levels, thus providing a higher degree of confidence prior to entering the market.

DISCLAIMER

We wish to emphasize that spot and futures currency trading may not be suited to everyone's disposition. All investors must be keenly aware of the risks involved and of the consequences of poor trading habits and/or mismanaged resources. Neither the publisher nor the author is liable for any losses incurred by readers while trading currencies.

PART 1
Currency Markets

Chapter **1**
Spot Currencies

OVERVIEW

Foreign exchange is the simultaneous buying of one currency and selling of another. Currencies are traded through a broker or dealer and are executed in pairs, for example, the Euro and the U.S. dollar (EUR/USD) or the British pound and the Japanese yen (GBP/JPY).

The *foreign exchange market* (Forex) is the largest financial market in the world, with a volume of over $2 trillion daily. This is more than three times the total amount of the stocks, options, and futures markets combined.

Unlike other financial markets, the Forex spot market has no physical location, nor a central exchange. It operates through an electronic network of banks, corporations, and individuals trading one currency for another. The lack of a physical exchange enables the Forex to operate on a 24-hour basis, spanning from one time zone to another across the major financial centers. This fact has a number of ramifications that we will discuss throughout this book.

A *spot market* is any market that deals in the current price of a financial instrument. Futures markets, such as the Chicago Board of Trade (CBOT), offer commodity contracts whose delivery date may span several months into the future. Settlement of Forex spot transactions usually occurs within two business days.

CURRENCY PAIRS

Every Forex trade involves the simultaneous buying of one currency and the selling of another currency. These two currencies are always referred to as the *currency pair* in a trade.

BASE CURRENCY

The *base currency* is the first currency in any currency pair. It shows how much the base currency is worth, as measured against the second currency. For example, if the USD/CHF rate is 1.6215, then one U.S. dollar is worth 1.6215 Swiss francs. In the Forex markets, the U.S. dollar normally is considered the base currency for quotes, meaning that quotes are expressed as a unit of US$1 per the other currency quoted in the pair. The primary exceptions to this rule are the British pound, the Euro, and the Australian dollar.

QUOTE CURRENCY

The *quote currency* is the second currency in any currency pair. This is frequently called the *pip currency*, and any unrealized profit or loss is expressed in this currency.

PIPS AND TICKS

A *pip* is the smallest unit of price for any foreign currency. Nearly all currency pairs consist of five significant digits, and most pairs have the decimal point immediately after the first digit; that is, EUR/USD equals 1.2812. In this instance, a single pip equals the smallest change in the fourth decimal place, that is, 0.0001. Therefore, if the quote currency in any pair is USD, then one pip always equals 1/100 of a cent.

One notable exception is the USD/JPY pair, where a pip equals US$0.01 (one U.S. dollar equals approximately 107.19 Japanese yen). Pips sometimes are called *points*.

Just as a pip is the smallest price movement (the y axis), a *tick* is the smallest interval of time along the x axis that occurs between

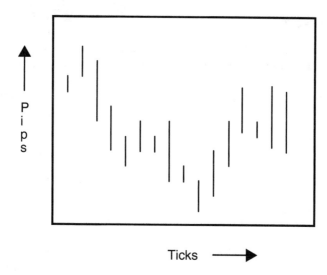

Figure 1-1 Pips versus Ticks Relationship.

two trades. (Occasionally, the term *tick* is also used as a synonym for *pip*.) When trading the most active currency pairs (such as EUR/USD and USD/JPY) during peak trading periods, multiple ticks may (and will) occur within the span of one second. When trading a low-activity minor cross-pair (such as the Mexican peso and the Singapore dollar), a tick may occur only once every two or three hours (Figure 1-1).

Ticks, therefore, do not occur at uniform intervals of time. Fortunately, most historical data vendors will group sequences of streaming data and calculate the open, high, low, and close over regular time intervals (1, 5, and 30 minutes, 1 hour, daily, and so forth).

BID PRICE

The *bid* is the price at which the market is prepared to buy a specific currency pair in the Forex market. At this price, the trader can sell the base currency. The bid price is shown on the left side of the quotation. For example, in the quote USD/CHF 1.4527/32, the bid price is 1.4527, meaning that you can sell one U.S. dollar for 1.4527 Swiss francs.

ASK PRICE

This *ask* is the price at which the market is prepared to sell a specific currency pair in the Forex market. At this price, the trader can buy the base currency. The ask price is shown on the right side of the quotation. For example, in the quote USD/CHF 1.4527/32, the ask price is 1.4532, meaning that you can buy one U.S. dollar for 1.4532 Swiss francs. The ask price is also called the *offer price*.

BID/ASK SPREAD

The difference between the bid price and ask price is called the *spread*. The *big-figure quote* is a dealer expression referring to the first few digits of an exchange rate. These digits often are omitted in dealer quotes. For example, a USD/JPY rate might be 117.30/117.35 but would be quoted verbally without the first three digits as 30/35.

The critical characteristic of the bid/ask spread is that it is also the *transaction cost* for a round-turn trade. *Round turn* means both a buy (or sell) trade and an offsetting sell (or buy) trade of the same size in the same currency pair. In the case of the EUR/USD rate above, the transaction cost is 3 pips (Figure 1-2).

FORWARDS AND SWAPS

Outright forwards are structurally similar to spot transactions in that once the exchange rate for a forward deal has been agreed, the confirmation and settlement procedures are the same as in the cash market. *Forwards* are spot transactions that have been held over 48 hours but less than 180 days when they mature and are liquidated at the prevailing spot price.

Transaction Cost = Ask Price − Bid Price

Figure 1.2 Calculating Transaction Costs.

Forex *swaps* are transactions involving the exchange of two currency amounts on a specific date and a reverse exchange of the same amounts at a later date. Their purpose is to manage liquidity and currency risk by executing foreign exchange transactions at the most appropriate moment. Effectively, the underlying amount is borrowed and lent simultaneously in two currencies, for example, by selling U.S. dollars for the Euro for spot value and agreeing to reverse the deal at a later date.

Since currency risk is replaced by credit risk, such transactions are different conceptually from Forex spot transactions. They are, however, closely linked because Forex swaps often are initiated to move the delivery date of a foreign currency originating from spot or outright forward transactions to a more optimal moment in time. By keeping maturities to less than a week and renewing swaps continuously, market participants maximize their flexibility in reacting to market events. For this reason, swaps tend to have shorter maturities than outright forwards. Swaps with maturities of up to one week account for 71 percent of deals, compared with 53 percent for outright forwards. For additional information, see www.aforextrust.com/spot-forex-forex-forwards-forex-swaps.htm.

Chapter 2
Currency Futures

FUTURES CONTRACTS

A *futures contract* is an agreement between two parties: a *short position*, the party who agrees to deliver a commodity, and a *long position*, the party who agrees to receive a commodity. For example, a grain farmer would be the holder of the short position (agreeing to sell the grain), whereas the bakery would be the holder of the long position (agreeing to buy the grain).

In every futures contract, everything is specified precisely: the quantity and quality of the underlying commodity, the specific price per unit, and the date and method of delivery. The price of a futures contract is represented by the agreed-on price of the underlying commodity or financial instrument that will be delivered in the future. For example, in the preceding scenario, the price of the contract is 5,000 bushels of grain at a price of $4 per bushel, and the delivery date may be the third Wednesday in September of the current year.

The Forex market is essentially a cash or spot market in which over 90 percent of the trades are liquidated within 48 hours. Currency trades held longer than this normally are routed through an authorized commodity futures exchange such as the International Monetary Market (IMM). IMM was founded in 1972 and is a division of the Chicago Mercantile Exchange (CME) that specializes in currency futures, interest-rate futures, and stock index futures, as well as options on futures. Clearinghouses (the futures exchange) and introducing brokers are subject to more stringent regulations from the Securities and Exchange Commission (SEC), Commodity Futures Trading Commission (CFTC), and National Futures Association (NFA) than the Forex spot market (see www.cme.com for more details).

It also should be noted that Forex traders are charged only a single transaction cost per trade, which is simply the difference between the current bid and ask prices. Currency futures traders are charged a round-turn commission that varies from brokerage house to brokerage house. In addition, margin requirements for futures contracts usually are slightly higher than the requirements for the Forex spot market.

CONTRACT SPECIFICATIONS

Table 2-1 presents a list of currencies traded through the IMM at the CME and their contract specifications.

CURRENCY TRADING VOLUME

Table 2-2 summarizes the trading activity of selected futures contracts in currencies, precious metals, and some financial instruments. The volume and open interest (OI) readings are not trading signals. They are intended only to provide a brief synopsis of each market's liquidity and volatility based on the average of 30 trading days.

U.S. DOLLAR INDEX

The U.S. Dollar Index (ticker symbol DX) is an openly traded futures contract offered by the New York Board of Trade (NYBOT). It is computed using a trade-weighted geometric average of the six currencies listed in Table 2-3.

Table 2-1 Currency Contract Specifications

Commodity	Contract size	Months	Hours	Minimum fluctuation
Australian dollar	100,000 AUD	H, M, U, Z	7:20–14:00	0.0001 AUD = $10.00
British pound	62,500 GBP	H, M, U, Z	7:20–14:15	0.0002 GBP = $12.50
Canadian dollar	100,000 CAD	H, M, U, Z	7:20–14:00	0.0001 CAD = $10.00
Euro	62,500 EUR	H, M, U, Z	7:20–14:15	0.0001 EUR = $6.25
Japanese yen	12,500,000 JPY	H, M, U, Z	7:00–14:00	0.0001 JPY = $12.50
Mexican peso	500,000 MXN	All months	7:00–14:00	0.0025 MXN = $12.50
New Zealand dollar	100,000 NZD	H, M, U, Z	7:00–14:00	0.0001 NZD = $10.00
Russian ruble	2,500,00 RUR	H, M, U, Z	7:20–14:00	0.0001 RUR = $25.00
South African rand	5,00,000 ZAR	All months	7:20–14:00	0.0025 ZAR = $12.50
Swiss franc	62,500 CHF	H, M, U, Z	7:20–14:15	0.0001 CHF = $12.50

Note: "Contract Size" represents one contract requirement, although some brokers offer minicontracts, usually one-tenth the size of the standard contract. "Months" identify the month of contract delivery. The tick symbols H, M, U, and Z are abbreviations for March, June, September, and December, respectively. "Hours" indicate the local trading hours in Chicago. "Minimum Fluctuation" represents the smallest monetary unit that is registered as 1 pip in price movement at the exchange and usually is one ten-thousandth of the base currency.

IMM currency futures traders monitor the U.S. Dollar Index to gauge the dollar's overall performance in world currency markets. If the U.S. Dollar Index is trending lower, then it is very likely that a major currency that is a component of the U.S. Dollar Index is trading higher. When a currency trader takes a quick glance at the price of the U.S. Dollar Index, it gives the trader a good feel for what is going on in the Forex market worldwide.

For traders who are interested in more details on commodity futures, we recommend Todd Lofton's paperbound book, *Getting Started in Futures* (Wiley, 1993).

Table 2-2 Futures Volume and Open Interest

Market	Ticker symbol	Exchange	Volume	OI (000)
S&P 500 E-Mini	ES	CME	489.1	377.9
Nasdaq 100 E-Mini	NQ	CME	237.6	158.4
Eurodollar	ED	CME	93.9	772.5
S&P 500	SP	CME	59.3	531.4
Eurocurrency	EC	CME	49.5	112.9
Mini-Dow	YM	CBOT	48.1	30.2
10-year T-note	TY	CBOT	43.1	676.4
Gold	GC	NYMEX	33.7	163.0
5-year T-note	FV	CBOT	29.6	582.8
30-year T-bond	US	CBOT	25.9	324.1
Japanese yen	JY	CME	18.6	132.1
Canadian dollar	CD	CME	18.0	64.2
Nasdaq 100	ND	CME	13.3	65.4
British pound	BP	CME	12.2	58.3
Silver	SI	NYMEX	10.0	84.2
Swiss franc	SF	CME	9.3	45.6
Mexican peso	ME	CME	8.8	30.5
Dow Jones	DJ	CBOT	8.7	29.5
Australian dollar	AD	CME	7.8	55.7
2-year T-note	TU	CME	7.0	108.6
Copper	HG	NYMEX	4.2	32.8

Source: Active Trader Magazine, January 16, 2004; www.activetradermag.com.

Table 2-3 U.S. Dollar Index Weights

Currency	Weight (%)
Euro	57.6
Japanese yen	13.6
British pound	11.9
Canadian dollar	9.1
Swedish krona	4.2
Swiss franc	3.6

PART 2
Technical Analysis

Chapter **3**
Pattern Recognition

OVERVIEW

Probably the most successful and most used means of making decisions and analyzing Forex markets is technical analysis. The difference between technical analysis and fundamental analysis is that technical analysis is applied only to the price action of the market. While fundamental data often can provide only a long-term forecast of exchange-rate movements, technical analysis has become the primary tool to analyze and trade short-term price movements successfully, as well as to set profit targets and stop-loss safeguards, because of its ability to generate price-specific information and forecasts. Technical analysts are by nature chart mongers. The more charts there are, the better is the forecast.

Historically, technical analysis in the futures markets has focused on the six price fields available during any given period of time: open, high, low, close, volume, and open interest. Since the Forex market has no central exchange, it is very difficult to estimate the latter two fields, volume and open interest. In this section, therefore, we will limit our analysis to the first four price fields.

In this section, the technical analysis methods have been categorized not only be the underlying techniques used but also by the type of output that each category generates. We will begin this summary with *pattern recognition*, probably the most popular and easiest to use technique within the technical analysis family. This method involves scanning a raw open-high-low-close (OHLC) chart (such as a vertical bar chart or a candlestick chart) from left to right searching for identifiable price formations.

Technical analysis consists primarily of a variety of technical studies, each of which can be interpreted to predict market direction or to generate buy and sell signals. Many technical studies share one common important tool: a price-time chart that emphasizes selected characteristics in the price motion of the underlying security. One great advantage of technical analysis is its "visualness."

IDENTIFYING PRICE FORMATIONS

Proper identification of an ongoing trend can be a tremendous asset to a trader. However, the trader also must learn to recognize recurring chart patterns that disrupt the continuity of trend lines. Broadly speaking, these chart patterns can be categorized as *reversal patterns* and *continuation patterns*.

REVERSAL PATTERNS

Reversal patterns are important because they inform the trader that a market entry point is unfolding or that it may be time to liquidate an open position. Figures 3-1 through 3-4 display the most common reversal patterns.

CONTINUATION PATTERNS

A continuation pattern implies that while a visible trend was in progress, it was interrupted temporarily and then continued in the

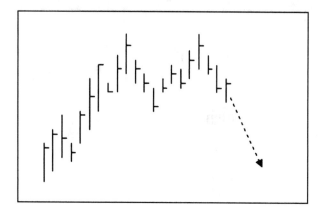

Figure 3-1 Double Top.

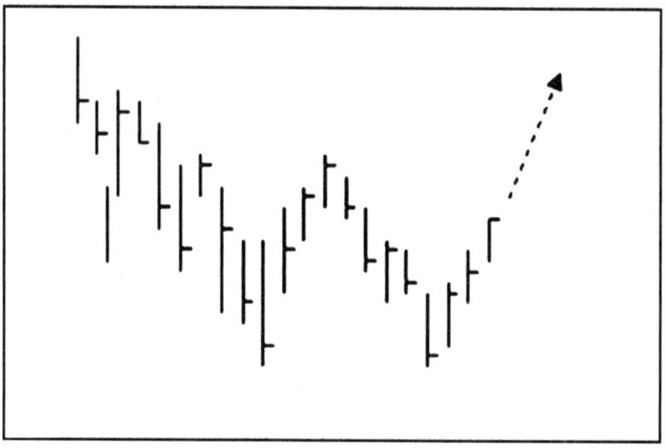

Figure 3-2 Double Bottom.

direction of the original trend. The most common continuation patterns are shown in Figures 3-5 through 3-9.

The proper identification of a continuation pattern may prevent a trader from entering a new trade in the wrong direction or from exiting a winning position too early.

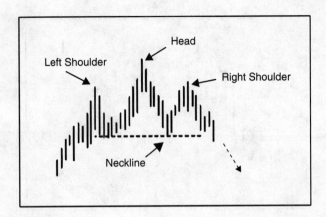

Figure 3-3 Head and Shoulders Top.

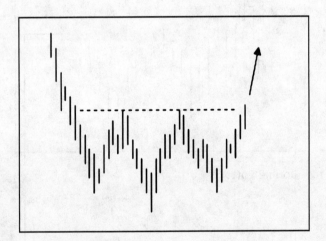

Figure 3-4 Head and Shoulders Bottom.

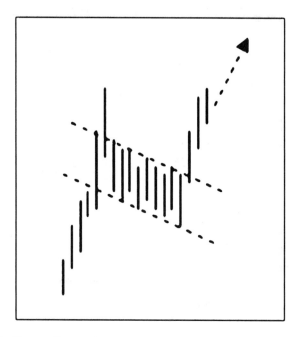

Figure 3-5 Flag or Pennant.

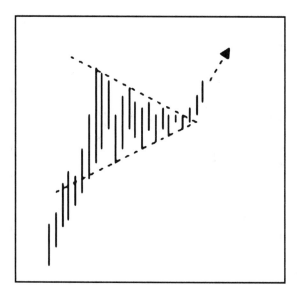

Figure 3-6 Symmetrical Triangle.

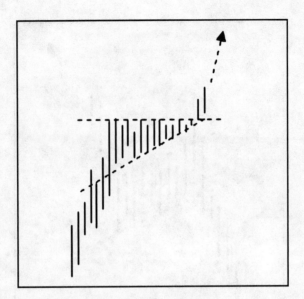

Figure 3-7 Ascending Triangle.

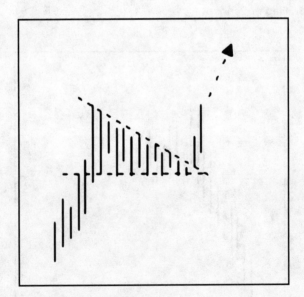

Figure 3-8 Descending Triangle.

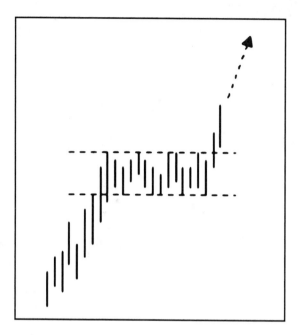

Figure 3-9 Rectangle.

Chapter 4
Econometric Models

OVERVIEW

Within the technical analysis family, econometric models are unique because they belong to the only category that generates a continuous stream of discrete numeric values as the forecast. For example, if the analyst has determined that a particular time series exhibits distinctly linear properties, then the following linear regression model should be used:

$$Y(x) = Ax + B + \varepsilon$$

where

x = the independent variable, time
$Y(x)$ = the dependent variable, the price at time index x
A = the slope
B = the intercept
ε = the error factor whose sum approximates zero

By solving for the regression coefficients A and B, the trader can estimate the next value in the time series $Y(\cdot)$ by incrementing the value of x in the linear model.

SIMPLE SINUSOIDAL MODEL

If security prices were not cyclical, they would tend to go off the top or bottom of the charts. This alone justifies the examination of a simple sinusoidal model. The current method identifies the most dominant sinusoidal in the time series using the conventional model:

$$Y(x) = A * \cos(x * \theta) + B * \sin(x * \theta) + \mu$$

where
x = the independent variable, time
$Y(x)$ = the dependent variable, the price at time index x
A = cosine amplitude
B = sine amplitude
θ = frequency, expressed as cycles per time unit
μ = the arithmetic mean of the time series

The crux of this regression is based on a fundamental trigonometric identity, specifically the following multiple-angle relationship:

$$\cos n\theta = 2 \cos\theta \cos(n-1)\theta - \cos(n-2)\theta$$

Once the frequency has been isolated and extracted, the two amplitudes can be calculated relatively simply.

Unfortunately, very few security time series exhibit a distinct single-cycle property for prolonged periods of time. However, the sinusoidal regression may be applied iteratively. That is, calculate the primary cycle coefficients, and remove that cycle from the original time series. Then perform the regression a second or third time.

FOURIER TRANSFORM

The fast Fourier transform is another popular method among technical analysts for extracting cycles from a time series. The basic assumption is that any (well-behaved) curve can be approximated as the sum of a finite number of sinusoidals and is based on the following Fourier series:

$$Y_x = A_0/2 + \Sigma A_n \cos(n\pi x/L) + \Sigma B_n \sin(n\pi x/L)$$

The transform operations calculate the values for the cosine amplitudes A and the sine amplitudes B in a similar fashion to the simple trigonometric regression above. Most analysts prefer to download an Internet utility to handle the complexities rather than code it themselves. Traders who are interested in more details should refer to *Fourier Analysis,* by Murray R. Spiegel, in the Schaum Outline Series (1974).

AUTOREGRESSION

The premise behind autoregressive methods is that previous values in the time series directly influence the current value in the time series. Mathematically, this can be expressed as

$$Y_{x+1} = AY_x + BY_{x-1} + CY_{x-2} + \varepsilon$$

where
x = the time increment
$Y(x)$ = the price at time index x
A = the first regression coefficient
B = the second regression coefficient
C = the third regression coefficient
ε = the error factor, whose sum approximates zero

This equation infers that the time-series closing price on any given day is the sum of the closing prices on the three previous days, all adjusted by regression coefficients. The number of independent variables on the right side of the equation determines the *autoregressive order* of the model.

Autoregression has numerous supporters in the realm of technical analysis. It also has several variations and enhancements, such as the autoregressive integrated moving-average (ARIMA) time-series model introduced by George Box and Gwilym Jenkins in the early 1970s. This model frequently is designated as the ARIMA(p, d, q) model, where p is the autoregressive order, d is differencing order, and q is the moving-average order. Traders interested in more information should refer to Box and Jenkins' book, *Time Series Analysis: Forecasting & Control* (Prentice-Hall, 1994). Readers who prefer a less advanced compendium should start with *The Analysis of Time Series: An Introduction*, by Chris Chatfield (CRC Press, 2003).

OTHER ECONOMETRIC MODELS

There exist a number of other econometric models that have been applied to financial time series. For example, the Holt-Winters model is a combination of a linear trend model and a seasonal model. A recent addition to time-series analysis is the generalized autoregressive conditional heteroskedacity model (GARCH), which attempts to improve on the ARIMA model by incorporating skew analysis of the data.

In addition, several statistical regression models (such as logistical and exponential) have been performed on securities data, but most return low correlation coefficients except over very short periods of time. See Chatfield's book (referenced above) for further details.

Chapter 5
Crossover Trading Systems

OVERVIEW

Crossover trading systems consist of various indicators and oscillators and are unique in the technical analysis of security prices. Rather than predicting future numeric values, they signal a particular market action to execute, such as (1) initiate a long position, (2) initiate a short position, (3) liquidate a long position, (4) liquidate a short position, (5) reverse a long position equivalent to (3) and (2), or reverse a short position equivalent to (4) and (1).

MOVING AVERAGES

Moving averages (MAs) are an important instrument used to study trends and generate market entry and exit signals. An MA is the arithmetic mean of the closing prices over a given period. The longer the period studied, the weaker is the magnitude of the moving-average curve. The number of closes in the given period is called the *moving-average index*. Market signals are generated by calculating the residual-difference value:

$$\text{Residual} = \text{close}(x) - \text{MA}(x)$$

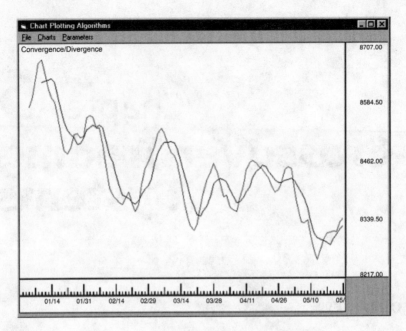

Figure 5-1 Daily Close with Five-day Moving Average.

In the chart shown in Figure 5-1, the curve with higher peaks and lower valleys is the daily close, whereas the smoother curve is a five-day moving average of the closes.

In the chart shown in Figure 5-2, called a *moving-average convergence/divergence (MACD) histogram,* the following signals are triggered:

1. When the residual difference rises above zero, a buy signal is generated.

2. When the residual difference falls below zero, a sell signal is generated.

A significant refinement to this residual-difference method, called *moving-average convergence/divergence* (MACD), involves the use of two moving averages. When the MA with the shorter MA index, called the *oscillating MA index,* crosses above the MA with the longer MA index, called the *basis MA index,* a sell signal is generated.

$$\text{MACD residual} = \text{basis MA}(x) \ \text{oscillating MA}(x)$$

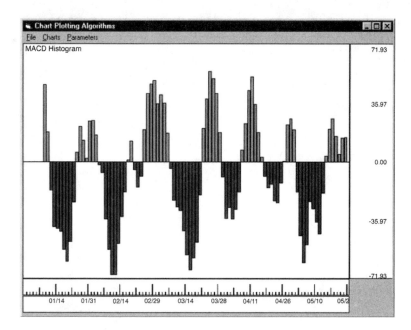

Figure 5-2 Residual Difference.

The reliability of the MACD method depends ultimately on the MA indices chosen. These two indices can be optimized by a computer program that performs a brute-force search for the most profitable parameters on the most recent daily closes. However, as market conditions change in the underlying time series, the indices must be adjusted accordingly.

It should be noted that some traders prefer to use exponentially smoothed moving averages rather than arithmetically smoothed moving averages, although this is usually a subjective decision on the part of the investor. In addition, we note that the MACD method is credited to Gerald Appel in the early 1960s in his book, *Technical Analysis: Power Tools for Active Investors* (Prentice-Hall, 1961).

RELATIVE STRENGTH INDEX

The relative strength index (RSI) was introduced by J. Welles Wilder in the June 1978 issue of *Commodities* (now known as

Figure 5-3   Relative strength Index.

Futures) magazine and later in his book, *New Concepts in Technical Trading* (Trend Research, 1978). The index is designed to follow the momentum of price as an oscillator that ranges between 0 and 100. The index tracks recent price to itself and therefore is a measure of velocity.

RSI is a front-weighted momentum indicator that measures a commodity's price relative to its past performance, and therefore, it gives a better velocity reading than other indicators. RSI is less affected by sharp rises or drops in a commodity's price performance. Thus it filters out some of the white noise in a security's trading activity (Figure 5-3).

The RSI formula is as follows:

$$\text{RSI} = 100 - [100 / (1 - U/D)]$$

where
U = average of up closes
D = average of down closes

For a nine-day RSI calculation, the following steps are involved:

1. Add the closing values for the up days, and divide this total by 9.
2. Add the closing values for the down days, and divide this total by 9.
3. Divide the up-day average by the down-day average. Store this as the RS factor in the formula.
4. Add 1 to the RS factor.
5. Divide 100 by the number arrived at in step 4.
6. Subtract the number arrived at in step 5 from 100.

Repeat steps 1 through 6 for day number 10. Drop day number 1 from the calculation.

Wilder originally proposed a 14-day RSI and later a 9- and a 25-day period. In modern times, this index can be optimized by a brute-force software program.

RSI values range from 1 to 100. Traditionally, buy signals are triggered at 30, and sell signals are triggered at 70. However, many analysts are now using 20 for buy signals and 80 for sell signals. RSI lends itself to support and resistance studies such as trend-line penetration and price patterns. Overbought and oversold conditions are suppose to be an asset in interpreting the RSI, but as you can see, overbought and oversold conditions do poorly in a strong trending environment.

The RSI shows whether a currency is overbought or oversold. Overbought indicates an upward market trend because the financial operators are buying a currency in the hope of further rate increases. Sooner or later, saturation will occur because the financial operators have already created a long position. They show restraint in making additional purchases and try to make a profit. The profits made can very quickly lead to a change in the trend or at least a consolidation.

Oversold indicates that the market is showing downward trend conditions because the operators are selling a currency in the hope of further rate falls. Over time, saturation will occur because the financial operators have created short positions. They then limit their sales and try to compensate for the short positions with profits. This can rapidly lead to a change in the trend.

STOCHASTIC OSCILLATORS

In a strictly mathematical sense, the term *stochastic* signifies a process involving a randomly determined sequence of observations, each of which is considered as a sample of one element from a probability distribution. In technical analysis, the term has evolved to signify an indicator that compares the current close with the highest high and the lowest low over a predetermined number of days.

The stochastic oscillator was developed by George C. Lane in the late 1950s. It is used most commonly to identify overbought and oversold conditions, as well as divergence between the oscillator and the price. The original stochastic plot consisted of two lines. The curve with higher peaks and lower valleys is referred to as $\%K$, and the other (more smoothed) line is called $\%D$ (Figure 5-4).

The stochastic oscillator compares where a security's price closed relative to its price range over a given time period. The basic formula is as follows:

$$\%K = 100(C - L)/(H - L)$$

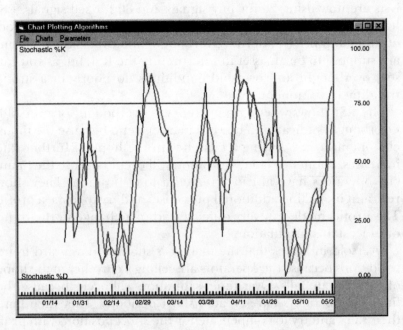

Figure 5-4   Stochastic Oscillators.

where
> C = current close
> H = highest high over given period of time
> L = lowest low over same period of time

The full stochastic oscillator has four variables:

1. *%K periods.* This is the number of time periods used in the stochastic calculation.

2. *%K slowing periods.* This value controls the internal smoothing of %K. A value of 1 is considered a fast stochastic; a value of 3 is considered a slow stochastic.

3. *%D periods.* This is the number of time periods used when calculating a moving average of %K. The moving average is called %D and usually is displayed as a dotted line on top of %K.

4. *%D method.* The smoothing method (i.e., exponential, simple, time series, triangular, variable, or weighted) that is used to calculate %D.

To calculate a 10-day %K, first find the security's highest high and lowest low over the last 10 days. As an example, let's assume that during the last 10 days the highest high was 46, and the lowest low was 38, a range of 8 points. If today's closing price was 41, %K would be calculated as:

$$100 * (41-38)/(46-38) = 37.5\%$$

The 37.5 percent in this example shows that today's close was at the level of 37.5 percent relative to the security's trading range over the last 10 days. If today's close was 42, the stochastic oscillator would be 50 percent. This would mean that the security closed today at 50 percent, or the midpoint, of its 10-day trading range.

This example used a %K slowing period of one day (no slowing). If you use a value greater than one, you average the highest high and the lowest low over the number of %K slowing periods before performing the division.

A moving average of %K then is calculated using the number of time periods specified in the %D periods. This moving average is called %D.

The stochastic oscillator always ranges between 0 and 100 percent. A reading of 0 percent shows that the security's close was the lowest price that the security has traded during the preceding x time periods. A reading of 100 percent shows that the security's close was the highest price that the security has traded during the preceding x time periods.

Popular interpretations of the stochastic oscillator include

- Buy when the oscillator (either %K or %D) falls below a specific level (e.g., 20) and then rises above that level. Sell when the oscillator rises above a specific level (e.g., 80) and then falls below that level.
- Buy when the %K line rises above the %D line, and sell when the %K line falls below the %D line.

Look for divergences, for example, where prices are making a series of new highs and the stochastic oscillator is failing to surpass its previous highs. Ways to use the stochastic oscillator as a confirming signal generator include

- A buy is indicated when the %K or %D falls below a specified level (typically 30) and then rises above that level. A sell is indicated when the line rises above a specified level (typically 70) and then goes below that level.
- A buy is indicated when the %K line rises above the %D line. A sell is indicated when the %K line falls below the %D line.

When prices are making new highs and the stochastic does not exceed its previous highs, a divergence occurs, often indicating a change in the current trend.

The buy/sell signals are triggered when the %K line crosses the %D line after the %D line has changed direction. At the bottom, the buy signal is generated. At the top, the sell signal is generated.

BOLLINGER BANDS

This indicator was developed by John Bollinger and is explained in detail in his book, *Bollinger on Bollinger Bands* (McGraw-Hill, 2001). The technique involves overlaying three bands (lines) on

Figure 5-5 Bollinger Bands.

top of an OHLC bar chart or a candlestick chart of the underlying security.

The center line is a simple arithmetic moving average of the daily closes using a trader-selected moving-average index. The upper and lowers bands are the running standard deviation above and below the central moving average. Since the standard deviation is a measure of volatility, the bands are self-adjusting: widening during volatile markets and contracting during calmer periods. Bollinger recommended 10 days for short-term trading, 20 days for intermediate-term trading, and 50 days for longer term trading. These values typically apply to stocks and bonds; thus shorter time periods will be preferred by commodity and currency traders (Figure 5-5).

Bollinger Bands require two trader-selected input variables: the number of days in the moving-average index and the number of standard deviations to plot above and below the moving average. Over 95 percent of all the daily closes will fall with three standard deviations of the mean of the time series. Typical values for the second parameter range from 1.5 to 2.5 standard deviations.

As with moving-average envelopes, the basic interpretation of Bollinger Bands is that prices tend to stay within the upper and lower bands. The distinctive characteristic of Bollinger Bands is that the spacing between the bands varies based on the volatility of the prices. During periods of extreme price changes (i.e., high volatility), the bands widen to become more forgiving. During periods of stagnant pricing (i.e., low volatility), the bands narrow to contain prices.

Bollinger notes the following characteristics of Bollinger Bands:

- Sharp price changes tend to occur after the bands tighten as volatility lessens.
- When prices move outside the bands, a continuation of the current trend is implied.
- Bottoms and tops made outside the bands followed by bottoms and tops made inside the bands call for reversals in the trend.
- A move that originates at one band tends to go all the way to the other band. This observation is useful when projecting price targets.

Bollinger Bands generally do not trigger buy and sell signals alone. They should be used with another indicator, usually the RSI. This is so because when the price touches one of the bands, it could indicate one of two things: a continuation of the trend or a reaction the other way. Thus Bollinger Bands used by themselves do not provide all of what technicians need to know, which is when to buy and sell. MACD can be used in conjunction with Bollinger Bands and the RSI.

OTHER CROSSOVER SYSTEMS

The techniques and methods just listed in no way represent all the crossover trading systems available to technical analysts. Numerous range and momentum oscillators also have been devised as crossover triggers, as well as several volume oscillators.

Chapter **6**
Wave Theory

OVERVIEW

Wave theory is one of the most intriguing and perplexing studies within the entire technical analysis complex. It is also the central subject of the remainder of this book.

WAVE CHARTS

Wave theory normally does not generate discrete numeric forecasts, as do the econometric models discussed previously. Nor does wave theory trigger specific market actions, as do the crossover trading systems.

Instead, wave theory converts the raw data into a series of alternating interconnected diagonal lines whose vertices accentuate local peaks and valleys based on the parameters of a reversal algorithm (Figure 6-1).

WAVE FORECASTING

The object of wave analysis is to discern the heights (y axis) and the widths (x axis) of subsequent waves based on mathematical ingenuity, ratio analysis, and the frequencies of preceding wave patterns called *cycles*. This is obviously an ambitious task, but given adequate data and resources, we feel that this is an achievable goal.

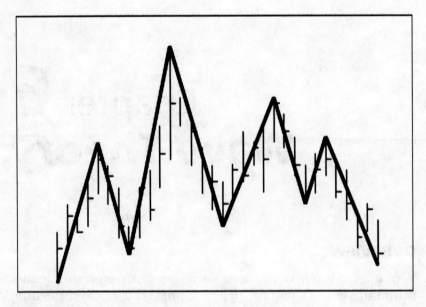

Figure 6-1   Simple Wave Chart.

CAVEAT

In addition to the four basic types of technical analysis described
in this part (i.e., pattern recognition, econometric models,
crossover trading systems, and wave theory), there exist other, less
frequently employed techniques. Unfortunately, some of these
involve such esoteric methods as astrology, numerology, and the
like. Let the trader beware.

PART 3
Reversal Charts

Chapter **7**
Point and Figure Charts

OVERVIEW

The point and figure chart is a member of the genre of charts normally referred to as *reversal charts* (Figure 7-1). A reversal chart is any chart that filters the raw OHLC data in order to accentuate significant *points of interest* while ignoring points of less interest. All technical analysts find peaks and valleys of great interest, whereas they find areas of lateral price movements less interesting. Peaks and valleys are those points of inflection where price directions reverse and the slope of an existing trend changes its arithmetic sign (minus to plus and plus to minus).

HISTORY

The point and figure chart (also called the *three-box reversal method*), created in the late nineteenth century, is roughly 15 years older than the bar chart and is probably the oldest Western method of charting prices in existence. Its roots date way back in trading lore, and it has been intimated that this method was used successfully by the legendary trader James R. Keene during the merger of U.S. Steel in 1901. Mr. Keene was employed by Andrew Carnegie to distribute ownership, because Carnegie refused to take stock as payment for

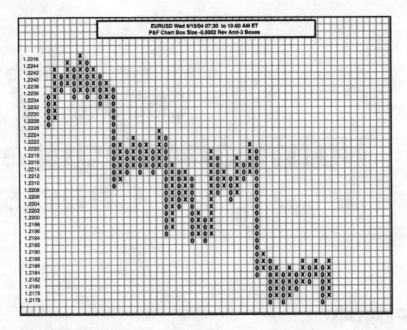

Figure 7-1 Point and Figure Chart.

his equity interest in the company. Keene, using point and figure charting and tape readings, managed to promote the stock and get rid of Carnegie's sizable stake without causing the price to crash.

The point and figure method derives its name from the fact that price is recorded using figures (X's and O's) to represent a point, hence point and figure. Charles Dow, the founder of the *Wall Street Journal* and the inventor of stock indexes, was rumored to be a point and figure user, and the practice of point and figure charting is alive and well today on the floor of the Chicago Board of Trade (CBOT). Its simplicity in identifying price trends, support, and resistance, and its ease of upkeep have allowed this method to endure the test of time, even in the age of Web pages, personal computers, and the information explosion.

ANATOMY

Price advances in a point and figure chart are represented as vertical columns of X's, whereas price declines are represented as columns of O's (Figure 7-2).

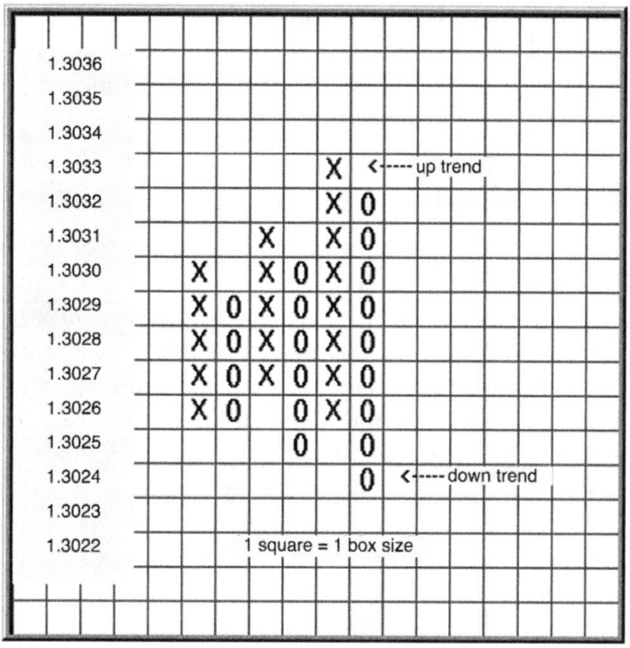

Figure 7-2   Point and Figure Chart Anatomy.

Two user-supplied variables are required to plot a point and figure chart, *box size* and *reversal amount.*

BOX SIZE

Traditionally, the minimum price unit is the smallest fractional price increment that a quote currency (or underlying security) can change. In the currency markets, this increment is a single pip. For example, if the EURUSD currency pair is currently trading at 1.2451, a single pip is 0.0001 USD.

There are three cases where a box size greater than 1 pip might be used. One such case is when the parity rate between two currencies is very wide and causes a very large bid/ask spread. For example, if the bid/ask spread (transaction cost) for the EURCZK currency pair is 350 koruny, then a 1-pip box size will have very negligible filtering power.

A second reason for using a box size greater than 1 pip occurs when performing historical analysis and a longer time frame is being analyzed. In this case, the analyst probably will be scrutinizing major reversals and may have little interest in minor reversals. This pertains more to position traders than to session or day traders.

REVERSAL AMOUNT

The reversal amount is the number of boxes necessary to plot a reversal in price direction. For instance, if the current trend is upward and the reversal amount is set at three boxes, then a decline of three box units must be reached before the downward movement is plotted. If, instead, a new price continues in the same direction as the existing trend, then single boxes are added automatically to the last extreme (either a peak or a valley).

It is the interaction between the box size and the reversal amount that triggers the reversal mechanism in the reversal algorithm necessary to plot new columns of X's and O's while ignoring lateral price movements.

There is one final case for increasing box size. If an analyst, for whatever reasons, has become very partial to one specific reversal amount, it is possible to increase the box size instead of the reversal amount when market conditions change.

For example, a three-box reversal amount is favored by many traders. If traders wish to filter out some of the minor reversals, they can increase either the reversal amount or the box size. However, keep in mind that although an algorithm with a 2-pip box size and a three-box reversal amount will generate results very similar to those of an algorithm with a 1-pip box size and a six-box reversal amount, they will not be identical. This requires some reflection. The reason is that when you plot a continuation of an existing trend, smaller distances can be plotted when a smaller box size is used.

A detailed study of point and figure charts can be found in *Forex Chartist's Companion,* by Archer and Bickford (Wiley, 2007).

Chapter **8**
Renko Charts

OVERVIEW

The renko charting method is thought to have acquired its name from *renga*, which is the Japanese word for "bricks." Renko charts are similar to three-line-break charts except that in a renko chart, a line (or *brick*, as they are called) is drawn in the direction of the prior move only if prices move by a minimum amount (i.e., the box size). The bricks are always equal in size. For example, in a five-unit renko chart, a 20-point rally is displayed as four five-unit-tall renko bricks.

ANATOMY

Basic trend reversals are signaled with the emergence of a new white or black brick. A new white brick indicates the beginning of a new uptrend. A new black brick indicates the beginning of a new down-trend (Figure 8-1).

Since the renko chart is a trend-following technique, there are times when renko charts produce whipsaws, giving signals near the end of short-lived trends. However, the expectation with a trend-following technique is that it allows the trader to ride the major portion of significant trends. Since a renko chart isolates the underlying price trend by filtering out the minor price changes, renko charts also can be very helpful when determining support and resistance levels (Figure 8-2).

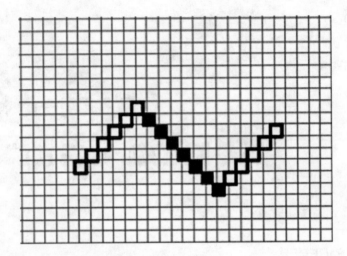

Figure 8-1   Renko Peak and Valley Chart.

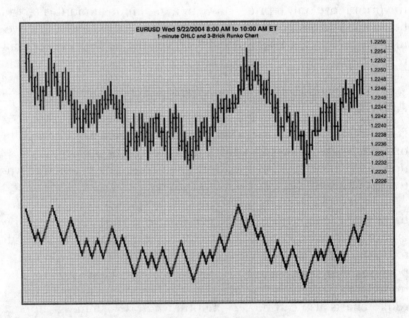

Figure 8-2   OHLC With Three-Brick Renko Chart.

BRICK SIZE

Brick size is analogous to box size in a point and figure chart and determines the minimum price change to display. Renko charts do not have an equivalent to point and figure reversal amount because the default is always one brick. To filter out white noise, simply increase the brick size.

ALGORITHM

To draw renko bricks, today's close is compared with the high and low of the previous brick (white or black):

- If the closing price rises above the top of the previous brick by at least the box size, one or more white bricks are drawn in new columns. The height of the bricks is always equal to the box size.
- If the closing price falls below the bottom of the previous brick by at least the box size, one or more black bricks are drawn in new columns. Again, the height of the bricks is always equal to the box size.
- If prices move more than the box size but not enough to create two bricks, only one brick is drawn. For example, in a two-unit renko chart, if the prices move from 100 to 103, only one white brick is drawn from 100 to 102. The rest of the move, from 102 to 103, is not shown on the chart.

Note that the x axis does not represent time in a perfectly linear fashion because there is always one x-axis unit per brick. If the background grid is set at 1×1, then vertices also will be at right angles.

REFERENCES

Nison, Steven, *Beyond Candlesticks: More Japanese Charting Techniques Revealed*   (New York: Wiley, 1994).
Nison, Steven, *Japanese Candlestick Charting Techniques* (New York: Hall, 1991).
www. linnsoft.com/welcome/charts.htm.

Chapter **9**
Swing Charts

OVERVIEW

A swing chart is another member of a genre of charts referred to as *reversal charts*. As stated in Chapter 7, a reversal chart is any chart that filters raw data in order to accentuate significant points of interest while ignoring points of less interest. All technical analysts find peaks and valleys of great interest, whereas they find areas of lateral price movements less interesting. Peaks and valleys are those points of inflection where price directions reverse and the slope of an existing trend changes its arithmetic sign (minus to plus and plus to minus) (Figure 9-1).

DEFINITIONS

In this book, we prefer to use the original terms of trader/ theoretician R. N. Elliott to avoid any unnecessary confusion with terms used by other swing analysts.

- A *wave* is a single straight line in a swing chart. Waves are always diagonal lines with positive or negative slope, never perfectly horizontal or vertical.

- A *peak* is the point of intersection between an upward wave on the left and a downward wave on the right. This represents a local maximum in the raw data.

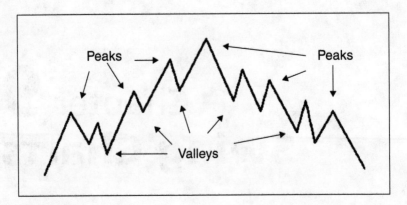

Figure 9-1   Peaks and Valleys.

- A *valley* (or *trough*) is the point of intersection between a downward wave on the left and an upward wave on the right. This represents a local minimum in the raw data.
- A *cycle* is a series of adjacent interconnected waves depicting specific price formations.

To convert a sequence of raw tick data or OHLC interval data to swing data, a swing-reversal algorithm is employed in which two user-supplied variables must be initialized, the *minimum fluctuation unit* and the *minimum reversal amount*.

MINIMUM FLUCTUATION UNIT

Traditionally, the *minimum price unit* is the smallest fractional price increment that a quote currency (or underlying security) can change. This is very similar to box size in point and figure charting. In the currency markets, this increment is a single pip. For example, if the EURUSD currency pair is currently trading at 1.2451, a single pip is 0.0001 USD.

There are three cases where a minimum fluctuation unit greater than 1 pip might be used. One such case is when the parity rate between two currencies is very wide and causes a very large bid/ask spread. For example, if the bid/ask spread (transaction cost) for the EURCZK currency pair is 350 koruny, then a 1-pip box size will have very negligible filtering power.

A second reason for using a box size greater than 1 pip occurs when performing historical analysis and a longer time frame is being analyzed. In this case, the analyst probably will be scrutinizing major reversals and may have little interest in minor reversals. This pertains more to long-term position traders rather than to session or day traders.

Lastly, a larger box size may be used to align peaks and valleys with the grid lines of the chart. This is purely a display preference, though.

MINIMUM REVERSAL AMOUNT

The *reversal amount* is the number of minimum fluctuation units necessary to plot a reversal in price direction. For instance, if the current trend is upward, and the reversal amount is set at three units, then a decline of three fluctuation units must be reached before the downward movement is plotted. If, instead, a new price continues in the same direction as the existing trend, then single boxes are added automatically to the last extreme (either a peak or a valley).

It is the interaction between the minimum fluctuation unit and the reversal amount that triggers the reversal mechanism in the swing algorithm necessary to plot peaks and valleys while ignoring lateral price movements.

There is one final case for increasing the minimum fluctuation unit. If an analyst, for whatever reasons, has become very partial to one specific reversal amount, it is possible to increase the minimum fluctuation unit instead of the reversal amount when market conditions change.

For example, a three-unit reversal amount is favored by many traders. If traders wish to filter out some of the minor swings, they can increase either the reversal amount or the minimum fluctuation unit. However, keep in mind that although an algorithm with a 2-pip unit size and a three-unit reversal amount will generate results very similar to an algorithm with a 1-pip unit size and a six-unit reversal amount, they will not be identical. This requires some reflection. The reason is that when you plot a continuation of an existing trend, smaller distances can be plotted.

SWING-REVERSAL ALGORITHM

Given the information and user-supplied variables generated earlier, we will now define the swing-reversal algorithm as follows (this algorithm assumes that we are using daily OHLC quotes as the input data rather than simply the closing prices):

```
Step 1: Initialize BoxSize and ReversalAmount
variables.

Step 2: Create a new variable called Direction.

Step 3: Create two array variables called Price
        and Time to hold the swing data.

Step 4: Set Price(1) = Close(1) and Time(1) = 1.
Step 5: If High(2) - Price(1) > BoxSize *
        ReversalAmount, then
            Set Price(2) = High(2).
            Set Time(2) = 2.
            Set Direction = UP.
        ElseIf Price(1) - Low(2) > BoxSize *
        ReversalAmount, then
            Set Price(2) = Low(2).
            Set Time(2) = 2.
            Set Direction = DOWN.
        Else
            Increment day number and repeat step 5
        End If

Step 6: Increment DayNo.
            If DayNo = Number of OHLC quotes, then
            Go to step 9.
    If Direction = DOWN, then
            Go to step 8.
        End If
```

```
  Step 7: If High(DayNo) - Price(Idx) > BoxSize,
then
                Set Price(Idx) = High(DayNo).
                Set Time(Idx) = DayNo.
            ElseIf Price(Idx) - Low(DayNo) > BoxSize *
            ReversalAmount, then
                Increment Swing Idx.
                Set Price(Idx) = Low(DayNo).
                Set Time(Idx) = DayNo.
                Set Direction = DOWN.
            End If
            Go to step 6.
  Step 8: If High(DayNo) - Price(Idx) > BoxSize *
            ReversalAmount, then
                Increment Swing Idx.
                Set Price(Idx) = High(DayNo).
                Set Time(Idx) = DayNo.
  Set Direction = UP.
            ElseIf Price(Idx) - Low(DayNo) > BoxSize,
then
                Set Price(Idx) = Low(DayNo).
                Set Time(Idx) = DayNo.
            End If
            Go to step 6.
  Step 9: Set Number of Swings = Swing Idx.
            Exit
```

At this point, the two swing arrays Price(·) and Time(·) have been populated with corresponding pairs of swing data.

TIME ALIGNMENT

Adherents of the point and figure charting method believe that the compression of time along the x axis is an advantage because the trader can focus solely on price movements. Proponents of swing charts, on the other hand, are more comfortable viewing the points of inflection (peaks and valleys) as they occur in real time. When a swing chart is displayed directly below an OHLC bar chart, the respective peaks and valleys will align vertically with the corresponding bar above. Swing charts also display the *velocity* of the market; that is, the slope of each wave determines how quickly the market is moving.

The point and figure chart versus swing chart debate is, in the final analysis, a matter of preference. Any swing chart can be readily "massaged" into a point and figure chart simply by converting the straight lines to columns of X's and O's. The converse, however, is not true because point and figure charts normally do not record the day numbers at the reversal vertices. We prefer the swing chart because in later chapters the number of time units in each wave will be used in numerous mathematical calculations.

PRACTICAL EXAMPLES

In the swing charts in Figures 9-2 through 9-5, the minimum fluctuation unit is set to 1 pip, whereas four different reversal amounts (3, 6, 9, and 12) are employed.

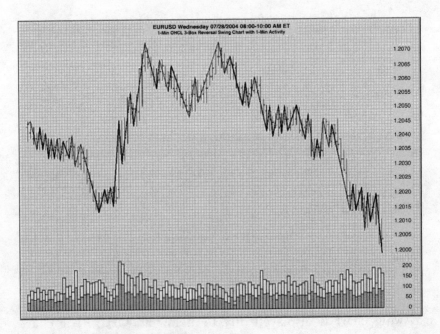

Figure 9-2   Three-box Reversal.

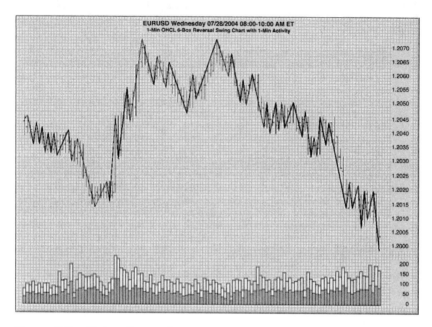

Figure 9-3 Six-box Reversal.

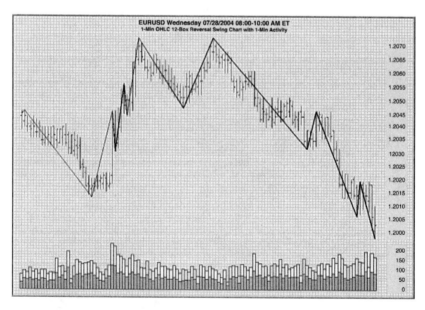

Figure 9-4 Nine-box Reversal.

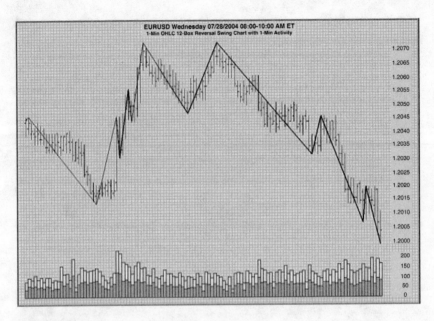

Figure 9-5 Twelve-box Reversal.

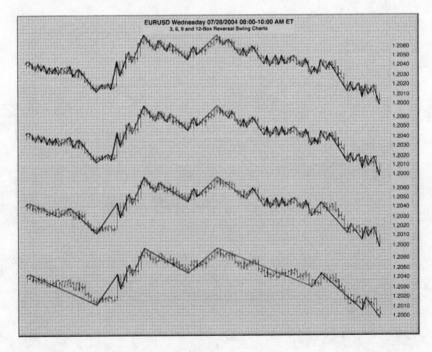

Figure 9-6 Composite Swing Chart.

As stated earlier, the number of waves generated by the swing algorithm has an inverse relationship with the reversal amount, i.e., as the reversal amount increases, the number of waves decreases, and vice versa (Table 9-1). Using the EURUSD currency pair for the time frame specified earlier, this equates to

Table 9-1 Inverse Relationship

Reversal amount	Swings
3	65
4	65
5	65
6	61
7	59
8	49
9	37
10	23
11	19
12	15
13	11
14	9
15	7

COMPOSITE SWING CHARTS

Figure 9-6, an aggregate of the preceding four swing charts, is included here so that traders can conceptually scrutinize the effect of different reversal amounts when using the same OHLC data.

USAGE

The advantages of comparing identical raw data time frames using different reversal amounts are twofold. First, any time traders view a single data set from different perspectives, there is a greater likelihood of discovering one particular nuance in one of the charts that may not be readily apparent in the sibling charts (more is better). Additionally, several trading systems are based on specific swing patterns, such as Elliott cycles and other patterns discussed later in this book. Some of these systems generate a discrete price estimate or at least predict price direction. Systematically varying the reversal amount allows traders to compare and log the forecasts at different levels, which adds an additional tier of reliability in the signal confirmation mechanism.

PART 4
Brief History of Wave Theory

Chapter 10
Origins of Wave Theory

OVERVIEW

The study of cycles dates back to ancient Greek, Babylonian, and Hindu mathematicians who all contributed to the discipline that we now called *trigonometry*, where the original applications were surveying and astronomy. In time, periodic functions, such as the sine and cosine functions, were developed to explain the nature of cycles.

The first major breakthrough in the cyclical study of time series occurred in 1822 when the French mathematician Joseph Fourier published his treatise entitled, *Analytical Theory of Heat*, which described his discoveries on the sinusoidal diffusion of heat transfer. This has evolved into a forecasting method presently referred to as the *discrete Fourier transform*. Many contemporary traders use Fourier analysis regularly as an integral component of their trading systems.

CHARLES DOW

Charles Henry Dow (1851–1902) was an American journalist who cofounded Dow Jones & Company and the *Wall Street Journal*, which became the most respected financial publication in the world.

Dow began his career in journalism at age 21 as a reporter with the *Daily Republican* in Springfield, MA. In 1875, he left Springfield to join the *Morning Star* and *Evening Press* in Providence, RI, where he met Edward Jones.

Dow relocated to New York City in 1879 and later joined the Kiernan News Agency, a firm that delivered handwritten news to banks and brokerage houses. By coincidence, Jones also had left the Providence *Morning Star* for the Kiernan News Agency. In November 1882, Dow and Jones formed Dow Jones & Company. Their first office was at 15 Wall Street, adjacent to the stock exchange. The first edition of the *Wall Street Journal* appeared July 8, 1889, with Dow as editor.

DOW JONES INDUSTRIAL AVERAGE

In the late nineteenth century, Dow identified financial markets as bull markets and bear markets, the upper and lower regions of a business cycle, respectively. Much of Dow's works focused on the performance of a single stock or security in relation to composite industry indexes, for which Dow is also credited. This performance index, now called a stock's *beta*, is the security's slope divided by an aggregate market slope as derived from two ordinary least squares (OLS) linear regressions.

First published on May 26, 1896, the Dow Jones Industrial Average (DJIA) represented the average of 12 stocks from various important American industries. Of those original 12, only General Electric remains part of the average today. The other 11 are listed in Table 10-1.

When it was first published, the DJIA stood at 40.94. It was computed as a direct average by first adding up stock prices of its components and then dividing by the number of stocks. In 1916, the number of stocks in the DJIA was increased to 20 and in 1928, finally to 30. On November 14, 1972, the average closed above 1,000 (1,003.16) for the first time. The DJIA currently consists of the 30 companies listed in Table 10-2.

The exact weighting coefficients for each stock component are published daily by Dow Jones.

Table 10-1   First Dow Jones Industrial Average

American Cotton Oil Company, a predecessor of Best Foods
American Sugar Company, now Amstar Holdings
American Tobacco Company, broken up in 1911
Chicago Gas Company, bought by Peoples Gas Light &
  Coke Co. in 1897
Distilling & Cattle Feeding Company, now Millennium
  Chemicals
Laclede Gas Light Company, still in operation as
  The Laclede Group
National Lead Company, now NL Industries
North American Company (Edison), electric company
  broken up in the 1950s
Tennessee Coal, Iron and Railroad Company, bought by
  U.S. Steel in 1907
U.S. Leather Company, dissolved in 1952
United States Rubber Company, bought by Michelin in 1990

DOW THEORY

Dow theory is a theory on stock price movements that provides the basis for technical analysis. The theory was derived from 255 *Wall Street Journal* editorials written by Dow. Following his death, William P. Hamilton, Charles Rhea, and E. George Schaefer organized and collectively represented "Dow theory" based on Dow's editorials. Dow himself never used the term *Dow theory*, though.

The six basic tenets of Dow theory, as summarized by Hamilton, Rhea, and Schaefer, are as follows:

1. *Markets have three trends.* To start with, Dow defined an uptrend (trend 1) as a time when successive rallies in a security price close at levels higher than those achieved in previous rallies and when lows occur at levels higher than previous lows. Downtrends (trend 2) occur when markets make lower lows and lower highs. It is this concept of Dow theory that provides the basis of technical analysis definition of a price trend. Dow described what he saw as a recurring theme in the market: Prices would move sharply in one direction, recede briefly in the opposite direction, and then continue in their original direction (trend 3).

2. *Trends have three phases.* Dow theory asserts that major market trends are composed of three phases: an accumulation phase,

Table 10-2 Most Recent Dow Jones Industrial Average

3M Co. (conglomerates, manufacturing)
ALCOA, Inc. (aluminum)
Altria Group, Inc. (tobacco, foods)
American International Group, Inc. (property and casualty insurance)
American Express Co. (credit services)
AT&T, Inc. (telecoms)
Boeing Co. (aerospace/defense)
Caterpillar, Inc. (farm and construction equipment)
Citigroup, Inc. (money-center banks)
Coca-Cola Co. (beverages)
E. I. du Pont de Nemours & Co. (chemicals)
Exxon Mobil Corp. (major integrated oil and gas)
General Electric Co. (conglomerates, media)
General Motors Corporation (automobile manufacturer)
Hewlett-Packard Co. (diversified computer systems)
Home Depot, Inc. (home-improvement stores)
Honeywell International, Inc. (conglomerates)
Intel Corp. (semiconductors)
International Business Machines Corp. (diversified computer systems)
JPMorgan Chase and Co. (money-center banks)
Johnson & Johnson, Inc. (consumer and health care products)
McDonald's Corp. (restaurant franchises)
Merck & Co., Inc. (drug manufacturers)
Microsoft Corp. (software)
Pfizer, Inc. (drug manufacturers)
Procter & Gamble Co. (consumer goods)
United Technologies Corp. (conglomerates)
Verizon Communications (telecoms)
Wal-Mart Stores, Inc. (discount, variety stores)
Walt Disney Co. (entertainment)

a public participation phase, and a distribution phase. The accumulation phase (phase 1) occurs when investors "in the know" are actively buying (selling) stock against the general opinion of the market. During this phase, the stock price does not change much because these investors are in the minority, absorbing (releasing) stock that the market at large is supplying (demanding). Eventually, the market catches on to these astute investors, and a rapid price change occurs (phase 2). This is when trend followers and other technically oriented investors participate. This phase continues until rampant speculation occurs. At this point, the astute investors begin to distribute their holdings to the market (phase 3).

3. *The stock market discounts all news.* Stock prices quickly incorporate new information as soon as it becomes available. Once news is released, stock prices will change to reflect this new information. On this point Dow theory agrees with one of the premises of the efficient-market hypothesis.

4. *Stock market averages must confirm each other.* In Dow's time, the United States was a growing industrial power. The United States had population centers, but factories were scattered throughout the country. Factories had to ship their goods to market, usually by rail. Dow's first stock averages were an index of industrial (manufacturing) companies and rail companies. To Dow, a bull market in industrials could not occur unless the railway average rallied as well, usually first. The logic is simple to follow: If manufacturers' profits are rising, it follows that they are producing more. If they produce more, then they have to ship more goods to consumers. Hence, if an investor is looking for signs of health in manufacturers, he or she should look at the performance of the companies that ship manufacturers' output to market, the railroads. The two averages should be moving in the same direction. When the performance of the averages diverges, it is a warning that change is in the air.

5. *Trends are confirmed by volume.* Dow believed that volume confirmed price trends. When prices move on low volume, there could be many different explanations why. An overly aggressive seller could be present, for example. However, when price movements are accompanied by high volume, Dow believed that this represented the true market view. If many participants are active in a particular security, and the price moves significantly in one direction, Dow maintained that this was the direction in which the market anticipated continued movement. To him, it was a signal that a trend is developing.

6. *Trends exist until definitive signals prove that they have ended.* Dow also believed that trends existed despite market noise. Markets might move in the direction opposite the trend temporarily, but they soon will resume the prior move. The trend should be given the benefit of the doubt during these reversals. Determining whether a reversal is the start of a new trend or a temporary movement in the current trend is not easy. Dow

theorists often disagree in this determination. Technical analysis tools attempt to clarify this, but they can be interpreted differently by different investors.

CONTROVERSY

As with many investment theories, there is conflicting evidence in support of and opposition to Dow theory. Alfred Cowles, in a study in *Econometrica* in 1934, showed that trading based on Dow's editorial advice would have earned less than a buy-and-hold strategy using a well-diversified portfolio. Cowles concluded that a buy-and-hold strategy produced 15.5 percent annualized returns from 1902 to 1929, whereas the Dow strategy produced annualized returns of 12 percent. After numerous studies supported Cowles over the following years, many academics stopped studying Dow theory, believing that Cowles' results were conclusive.

In recent years, however, some in the academic community have revisited Dow theory and question Cowles' conclusions. William Goetzmann, Stephen Brown, and Alok Kumar believe that Cowles' study was incomplete and that Dow theory produces excess risk-adjusted returns. Specifically, the absolute return of a buy-and-hold strategy was higher than that of a Dow theory portfolio by 2 percent, but the risk and volatility of the Dow theory portfolio were so much lower that the Dow theory portfolio produced higher risk-adjusted returns, according to their study. The Chicago Board of Trade also notes that there is growing interest in market-timing strategies such as Dow theory. Today, there is a plethora of investment strategies that claim to outperform a buy-and-hold strategy.

One key problem with any analysis of Dow theory is that the editorials of Charles Dow did not contain explicitly defined investing rules, so some assumptions and interpretations are necessary. Moreover, as with many academic studies of investing strategies, practitioners often disagree with academics.

Many technical analysts consider Dow theory's definition of a trend and its insistence on studying price action as the main premises of modern technical analysis. See www.en/wikipedia.org for further details on Dow theory.

DOW'S CONCEPT OF WAVES

Dow was one of the first market analysts to ascertain that markets fluctuate in more than one time frame at the same time:

> Nothing is more certain than that the market has three well-defined movements which fit into each other according to Dow.

The first fluctuation is the daily variation owing to local causes and the balance of buying and selling at that particular time (a ripple). The second movement covers a period ranging from days to weeks, averaging probably between six to eight weeks (a wave). The third move is the great swing covering anything from months to years, averaging between 6 to 48 months (a tide).

Nowadays, this multiple-cycle property is referred to as *fractality*, signifying that each individual wave in a cycle is composed of a set of smaller waves. Conversely, each wave is a component in a set of waves that compose an even larger wave. The concept of fractality will be examined in detail later in this book.

Chapter **11**
Gann Angles

W. D. GANN

William Delbert Gann (1878–1955) was one of the most successful stock and commodity traders in history. He has become a legend among open-minded traders the world over. He was famous not only for his legendary trading abilities but also for his financial market forecasts, which achieved a spectacular track record of accuracy.

Gann started trading in stocks and commodities in 1902, and in 1908, he moved to New York City, where he opened his own brokerage firm. His early trading career was far from successful, and he went bust more than once. This impelled him to look deeper into the markets. A unique analyst, his investigations led him to reach some startling conclusions, although controversy surrounds the claims of his trading successes and whether he did indeed reveal his real methods or took his secrets to the grave.

Gann reputedly made over $50 million in profits from his market forecasting and trading. In the early twentieth century, the U.S. dollar was worth far more than in the new millennium, so in current money this would be roughly $500 million. After five decades of success with his forecasting and trading, Gann moved to Florida, where he continued writing, publishing, teaching, and studying the markets until his death in June 1955.

Gann also was a prolific writer whose books include the following:

- *Tunnel Through the Air*
- *Truth of the Stock Tape*

- *Wall Street Stock Selector*
- *How to Make Profits Trading in Commodities*
- *45 Years in Wall Street*
- *Magic Word*
- *How to Make Profits Trading in Puts and Calls* (an early text on trading options)
- *Face Facts America*

BASIC ASSUMPTIONS

Gann based his predictions of price movements on three premises:

1. Price, time, and range are the only three factors to consider.
2. The markets are cyclical in nature.
3. The markets are geometric in their design and function.

By studying the past, we can predict the future. Gann believed that human nature was constant, and this showed up in repetitive price patterns that are identifiable and that therefore can be acted on to increase profit potential.

GEOMETRIC ANGLES

Gann designed several unique techniques for studying price charts. Central to his techniques was the concept of geometric angles in conjunction with time and price. Gann believed that specific geometric patterns and angles had unique characteristics that could be used to predict price action.

All Gann's techniques require that equal time and price intervals be used on the charts so that a rise/run of 1×1 will always equal a 45-degree angle.

INTERPRETATION

Gann believed that the ideal balance between time and price exists when prices rise or fall at a 45-degree angle relative to the time axis.

Table 11-1 Significant Gann Angles

1 × 8	82.5 degrees
1 × 4	75 degrees
1 × 3	71.25 degrees
1 × 2	63.75 degrees
1 × 1	45 degrees
2 × 1	26.25 degrees
3 × 1	18.75 degrees
4 × 1	15 degrees
8 × 1	7.5 degrees

This is also called a *1 × 1 angle* (i.e., prices rise one price unit for each time unit).

Gann angles are drawn between a significant bottom and top (or vice versa) at various angles. Deemed the most important by Gann, the 1×1 trend line signifies a bull market if prices are above the trend line or a bear market if below. Gann felt that a 1×1 trend line provides major support during an uptrend and that when the trend line is broken, it signifies a major reversal in the trend. Gann identified nine significant angles, with the 1×1 being the most important (Table 11-1).

Note that in order for the rise/run values (i.e., 1×1, 1×8, etc.) to match the actual angles (in degrees), the *x* and *y* axes must have equally spaced intervals. This means that one unit on the *x* axis (i.e., hours, days, weeks, months, or years) must be the same distance as one unit on the *y* axis. The easiest way to calibrate the chart is make sure that a 1×1 angle produces a 45-degree angle.

Gann observed that each of the angles can provide support and resistance depending on the trend. For example, during an uptrend, the 1×1 angle tends to provide major support. A major reversal is signaled when prices fall below the 1×1 angled trend line. According to Gann, prices then should be expected to fall to the next trend line (i.e., the 2×1 angle). In other words, as one angle is penetrated, expect prices to move and consolidate at the next angle. Gann developed several techniques for studying market action. These include Gann angles, Gann fans, Gann grids, and cardinal squares.

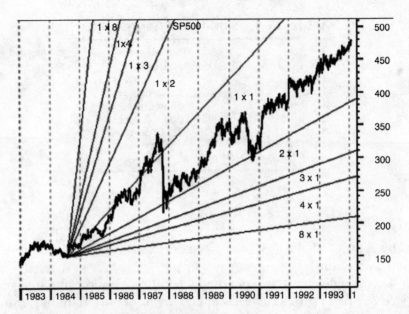

Figure 11-1 S&P 500 with Gann Angles.

A Gann fan displays lines at each of the angles that Gann identified. Figure 11-1 shows a Gann fan on the Standard & Poor's
(S&P) 500 Index.

Figure 11-2 shows the same S&P 500 data with a Gann grid. This
is an 80×80 grid on which each line is 1×1, and the lines are
spaced 80 weeks apart.

Gann based his market trading and forecasting methods on
time, as well as on price, and said repeatedly that time is most
important when it comes to analyzing and forecasting market
movements. Gann was able to determine not only what the turn-
ing point's price would be but also *when* it would occur. Being able
to forecast both time and price is the ultimate goal of technical
analysis, and many believe that it is impossible to do; the legend
of Gann, however, stands as the main opposition to this belief.
Another Gann aphorism is, "When you know how to use time with
price, you know how to trade."

Whether or not Gann revealed his real techniques and whether
or not *Tunnel Through the Air* did contain them in concealed form,

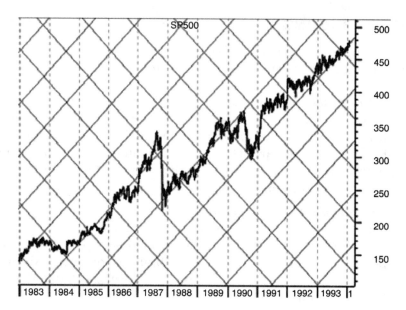

Figure 11-2 S&P 500 with Gann Grid.

the Gann techniques on the public record can be summarized as follows:

- Time and price are "the same." When they "square out," a major change of trend is due.

  Time is the most important factor. Do day/week counts of 30, 45, 60, 90, and 180.

- Resistance levels in both time and price are 25, 33, 50, 66, and 75 percent of the previous range. They can be extended (extrapolated) to 100, 150, and 200 percent.
- Trend lines work, and Gann can claim to have invented their use.

Gann believed that human nature is constant and that this shows up in repetitive price patterns that are identifiable and which therefore can be acted on to increase profit potential.

CONSTRUCTING GANN ANGLES

Predicting the market using Gann angles requires subjective judgment and practice. Here is the procedure:

1. *Determine the time units.* One common way to determine a time unit is to study the chart and look at the distances over which price movements occur. Then put the angles to the test and see how accurate they are. The intermediate-term time frame (one to three months) tends to produce the optimal number of patterns compared with short-term daily or multiyear charts.

2. *Determine the high or low from which to draw the Gann lines.* The most common way to accomplish this is to complement it with other forms of technical analysis, that is, Fibonacci levels or pivot points. Gann used what he called "vibrations" or "price swings." He determined these by analyzing charts using such theories as Fibonacci numbers.

3. *Decide which pattern to use.* The three most common patterns are the 1 × 1, the 1 × 2, and the 2 × 1. These are simply variations of the slope of the line. For example, the 1 × 2 is half the slope of the 1 × 1. The numbers simply indicate the number of units.

4. *Look for patterns.* The direction would be either downward and to the right from a high point or upward and to the right from a low point.

5. *Look for repeat patterns on the chart.* The basis of this technique is the premise that markets are cyclical.

The most common use for Gann angles when predicting the market is to indicate support and resistance levels. Many other trading methods use support and resistance lines, so what sets Gann's method apart from the rest?

Quite simply, predicting the market using Gann, angles adds a new dimension to support and resistance levels in that they can be diagonal. The optimal balance between time and price exists when prices move identically with time. This occurs when the Gann angle is at 45 degrees. In total, there are nine different Gann angles. When one of these trend lines is broken, the following angle will provide the next level of support or resistance.

Chapter **12**
Kondratiev Wave

NIKOLAI KONDRATIEV

Nikolai Dmitrievich Kondratiev (1892–1930) worked at the Agricultural Academy and Business Research Institute in Moscow. His research covered the major economies of the time: the United States, Great Britain, Germany, and France. He first considered wholesale prices and then looked at interest rates, wages, and foreign trade. Finally, he analyzed data on the production and consumption of coal, pig iron, and lead. He adjusted production figures to allow for population change and used a nine-year moving average to remove statistical noise. Kondratiev thought that the presence of a long wave was probable but could not be specific as to its cause, deeming it to be inherent in a capitalist economy. He postulated that it could arise because of the wearing out of capital goods, but he admitted that lack of reliable data curtailed conclusive verification. Numerous critics have attacked his methodology.

What was dangerously unacceptable to his Communist masters was the idea that there was an inherent self-correcting mechanism perpetuating capitalism. He was banished to the Gulag, where he was quickly condemned to solitary confinement. He became mentally ill and died.

Again, it was posthumous publication that drew attention to his work. His work was translated into English in 1935 (a German translation had been printed outside Russia in 1926, but it did not attract much attention at the time). There were two waves in wholesale prices during the nineteenth century in the United States of about 50 years each that conformed to Kondratiev's waveform. Both became identified as "Kondratiev cycles," and consequently, his work was given prominence in America.

Kondratiev was exiled to Siberia by Bolshevik officials who flatly rejected his conclusions. To the faithful, there could be only one falling phase of the capitalist economy, followed by the socialist revolution and the dictatorship of the proletariat. And following that, there was to be only one rising phase, leading to eternal bliss under Communism. Kondratiev died in the Gulag in 1930 at the age of 38. His work was later updated by other economists using his original methodology.

ECONOMIC CYCLES

A 50- to 60-year economic cycle was observed by a Dutchman, Van Gelderen, in 1913, although there is no evidence of a connection with Kondratiev. W. H. Beveridge (1879–1963) studied wheat prices back to the 1500s and is reputed to have deduced them back to 1260. He discovered many cycles, publishing his findings in 1921 and 1923 (three years earlier than Kondratiev). One of these cycles occurred every 50 to 60 years, with an average periodicity of 54 years.

The long-wave rhythm, which varies from 45 to 60 years, has attained its periodicity from averaging a wide distribution. It is widely known as the *Kondratiev wave* or, less elegantly, as the *K-wave*. Economists generally recognize four major cycles, or regular fluctuations, in the economy as follows:

1. Kitchin's short-wave cycle of average duration of 3 to 5 years, discovered in 1930

2. Juglar's cycle of average duration of 7 to 11 years, discovered in 1862

3. Kuznets' medium-wave cycle of average duration of 15 to 25 years, discovered in 1923

4. Kondratiev's long-wave cycle of average duration of 45 to 60 years, discovered in 1922.

J. Schumpeter, who served as president of the American Economic Society in the 1950s, was an outstanding student of economic cycles. He believed that the various cycles are interdependent, in contrast with the views of others such as Forrester, who believed that the cycles act independently of one another. Schumpeter baptized three of the four cycles by naming them after their discoverers.

Kondratiev identified three historic waves:

1. *First wave:* Rising phase from 1780–1790 to 1810–1817; falling phase from 1810–1817 to 1844–1851
2. *Second wave:* Rising phase from 1844–1851 to 1870–1875; falling phase from 1870–1875 to 1890–1896
3. *Third wave:* Rising phase from 1890–1896 to 1914–1920; falling phase started 1914–1920

After Kondratiev's death, economists found that the falling phase of the third wave ended in 1947–1948 and that there is a fourth wave: rising phase from 1947–1948 to 1973–1980; falling phase started 1973–1980.

CAUSES

Among economists, there is a lot of controversy as to why Kondratiev's long-wave cycle exists. Analysis of varying periods of economic prosperity, recession, depression, recovery, and improvement may provide a more understandable answer.

Much of the material in this chapter borders on the theoretical, and further information can be found at http:\en\wikipedia.org. We included this material because of the possibility that reversals in major economic cycles may have a direct or indirect influence on short- and medium-term trading. However, it is essentially general in nature and very difficult to apply to small-cap short-term spot currency trading. Nonetheless, knowledge is power.

Chapter **13**
Elliott Wave Theory

R. N. ELLIOTT

Ralph Nelson Elliott (1871–1948) had a successful career as a financial consultant to numerous railroad companies, a booming sector when he began his professional life just before the turn of the twentieth century. He was considered an expert in business planning, and his services were in very high demand. Such was his reputation that Elliott caught the eye of the U.S. State Department, which sent him to Nicaragua as an economic consultant, where he helped to reorganize the country's finances. It is said that one of his greatest talents in business was a shrewd eye for detail.

Training his meticulous eye on decades of market charts, Elliott discovered a persistent and recurring pattern that operated between market tops and bottoms. He theorized that these patterns, which he called *waves*, were a collective expression of investor sentiment, giving the market a distinct form and behavior. Through a use of measurements that he called *wave counting*, an analyst could forecast market turns with a high degree of accuracy.

After testing his theory over four years, Elliott organized his research into an essay that he titled, "The Wave Principle." This essay was published in book form on August 31, 1938, with the assistance of Charles Collins, a respected newsletter publisher who helped popularize Elliott wave analysis in its early years.

By the early 1940s, Elliott had fully developed his concept that the ebb and flow of human emotions and activities follow a natural progression governed by the laws of nature. He tied the patterns of collective human behavior to Fibonacci numbers and the Golden Ratio, a mathematical phenomenon known for centuries by mathematicians, scientists, artists, architects, and philosophers as one of nature's ubiquitous laws of form and progress.

Elliott then put together what he considered his definitive work, *Nature's Law: The Secret of the Universe.* This rather grandly titled monograph, which Elliott published at age 75, includes almost every thought he had concerning the theory of the wave principle. The book was published June 10, 1946, and the reported 1000 copies sold out quickly to various members of the New York financial community.

WAVE PATTERNS

Elliott believed that one business cycle consisted of a five-wave motive or impulse component and a three-wave corrective component. A motive or impulse pattern consists of five waves representing a distinct trend in one direction (Figure 13-1).

This pattern always satisfies the logical condition

Wave 1 > wave 2 < wave 3 > wave 4 < wave 5

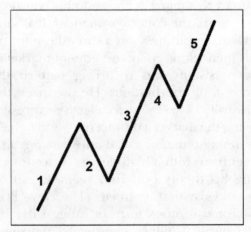

Figure 13-1 Impulse Pattern.

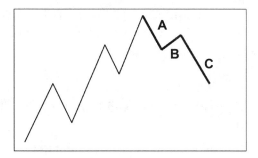

Figure 13-2 Corrective Pattern.

A corrective pattern consisting of three waves represents a countertrend in the opposite direction to its preceding impulse pattern (Figure 13-2).

The corrective pattern must obey the following constraint:

$$\text{Wave A} > \text{wave B} < \text{wave C}$$

Elliott identified several other wave patterns (such as zigzags, triangles, flats, and so on), but the impulse and corrective patterns are the most important when analyzing trends.

HERD PSYCHOLOGY

The following is a short description of herd psychology during each wave as it pertains to stock trades:

Wave 1. The stock makes its initial move upward. This is usually caused by a relatively small number of people that all of the sudden (for a variety of reasons real or imagined) feel that the price of the stock is cheap, so it is a perfect time to buy. This causes the price to rise.

Wave 2. At this point, enough people who were in the original wave consider the stock overvalued and take profits. This causes the stock to go down. However, the stock will not make it to its previous lows before it is considered a bargain again.

Wave 3. This is usually the longest and strongest wave. The stock has caught the attention of the mass public. More people find out about the stock and want to buy it. This causes the stock's price to go higher and higher. This wave usually exceeds the high created at the end of wave 1.

Wave 4. People take profits because the stock is considered expensive again. This wave tends to be weak because there are usually more people who are still bullish on the stock and are waiting to buy in the valleys.

Wave 5. This is the point that most people get on the stock and is most driven by hysteria. This is when the stock becomes the most overpriced. Contrarians start shorting the stock, which starts the ABC pattern.

TRADING TIMELINE

The motive phase contains five waves. The five waves may move up or down, that is, a bull or bear market.

The first wave is generally a tentative rally with only a small percentage of the traders participating. Elliott's rules state that wave 2 must retrace wave 1 by at least 20 percent, but it generally is a deep retracement of between 30 and 80 percent. Volume and volatility generally decline in wave 2 (Figure 13-3).

Wave 3 begins slowly with light to average volume, and it finally pushes toward the end of the previous wave 1. Many traders have placed stops at this level, thinking that the move is unsustainable. If wave 3 moves past the end of wave 1, these stops will be taken out, creating a gap and an increase in volume (Figure 13-4).

Traders who are skeptical of the move are adding shorts (in a bull move) or going long (in a bear move). This is the fuel that ignites the wave 3 impulse (Figure 13-5).

Stops placed above wave 1 are taken out, creating a gap and a surge in volume. Gaps and volume are indicative of a third wave in progress (Figure 13-6).

As the third-wave move gathers momentum and exceeds the previous wave 1 top (or bottom in a bear market), the stops are taken out, and gaps generally are left open. More traders are now ready to jump in and join the trend. Wave 3 accelerates, and volume increases.

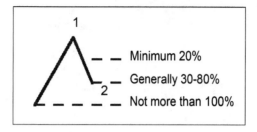

Figure 13-3   Second-Wave Retracement.

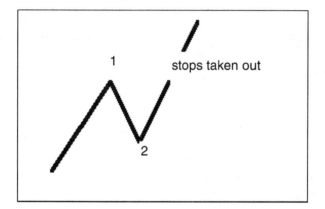

Figure 13-4   Third-Wave Rally.

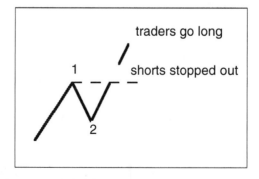

Figure 13-5   Third-Wave Shorts Stopped Out.

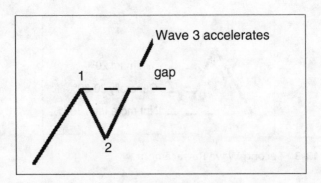

Figure 13-6   Third-Wave Accelerates.

Traders who got stopped out join the trend and add positions that further accelerate the third-wave impulse. The herd now has decided that the move is genuine and adds positions. As profit taking sets in, wave 4 begins.

Wave 2 usually exhibits massive selling with a deep retracement. Elliott rules state that wave 2 cannot retrace more than 100 percent of impulse wave 1. Wave 4 exhibits an orderly profit-taking decline. Traders who are still convinced that the trend has not changed begin "buying the dip" to get in on the next move, and wave 5 begins (Figure 13-7).

The fifth-wave rally is weaker and generally has less volume than the third-wave rally. New highs are made in the impulse fifth wave but with less strength. As the buying interest fades, the motive phase ends, and the corrective phase ensues. Additional information is available at www.wavemagician.com/elliottwave.htm.

WAVES WITHIN A WAVE

Elliott proposed that the waves existed at many levels, meaning that there could be waves within waves. Figure 13-8 shows how primary waves could be broken down into smaller waves.

This figure displays four of the eight waves as their component waves:

Wave 3 consists of a five-wave bull impulse cycle.

Wave 4 consists of a three-wave corrective cycle.

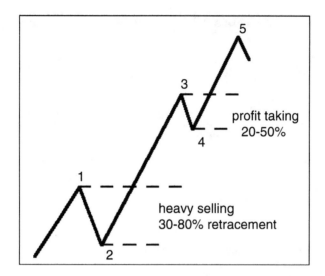

Figure 13-7 Completed Impulse Cycle.

Wave *A* consists of a five-wave bear impulse cycle.

Wave *B* consists of a three-wave corrective cycle.

Elliott assigned the nomenclature shown in Table 13-1 to the waves in order of descending size.

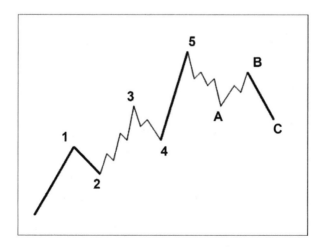

Figure 13-8 Waves within Waves.

Table 13-1   Cycle Names

1. Grand supercycle
2. Supercycle
3. Cycle
4. Primary
5. Intermediate
6. Minor
7. Minute
8. Minuette
9. Subminuette

The concept of waves within other waves dates back to Charles Dow and probably earlier. However, Dow believed that there were only three levels of wave composition. The scientific name for this phenomenon is *fractal geometry.*

RULES AND GUIDELINES

There are over 273 major rules and guidelines in the Elliott wave principle. Elliott rules must be obeyed in detail for a pattern to qualify as an Elliott wave or cycle. The guidelines do not have to be obeyed precisely. The more guidelines obeyed by an Elliott pattern, the higher is its probability of being correct.

A very brief summary of the rules governing a bull impulse cycle follows:

- No part of wave 2 can more than retrace wave 1.

- Wave 2 must retrace wave 1 by a minimum of 20 percent.

- The maximum time for wave 2 is nine times wave 1.

- Wave 3 must be longer than wave 2 in gross distance by price.

- Wave 3 and wave 1 cannot both have wave 5 failures.

- Wave 3 cannot be less than one-third of wave 1 by price.

- Wave 3 cannot be more than seven times wave 1 by price.

- The absolute maximum time limit for wave 3 is seven times wave 1.

A comprehensive list of the major rules and guidelines for the Elliott wave principle can be found at www.geocities.com/

WallStreet/Exchange/9807/Charts/SP500-Articles/EWRules.
htm#imprule.

USE

There are two immediate methods for applying Elliott wave theory
to a specific time frame in a given financial market. The first
requires identifying where the most recent price is located in the
current Elliott business cycle. This information allows the trader to
determine the direction and possible magnitude of the subsequent
wave in that cycle. Calculating the next-higher fractal wave level (i.e.,
the parent wave) offers the trader some confirmation if the parent
wave indicates a move in the same direction as the child wave.

The second method involves use of the Elliott wave oscillator based
on a standard moving-average convergence/divergence (MACD)
crossover method. Author and trader Perry Kaufman recommends
using a 5-period moving average for the oscillating moving-average
index and a 35-period moving average as the basis for the moving-
average index. Plotting the residual difference between the two
moving averages will highlight five peaks (or valleys) when a valid 5-3
wave pattern is in progress. This technique is described in detail at
www.investopedia.com/university/advancedwave/elliottwave3.asp.

Of course, there are several other methods for interpreting
Elliott wave results. For the serious trader interested in Elliott wave
analysis, we recommend *Elliott Wave Principle: Key to Market Behavior*
(New Classics Library, 1978), by Robert Prechter and A. J. Frost.

CAVEAT

A Google Internet search on "Elliott waves" generates over two million
matches, thus confirming the immense popularity of the system.
Elliott wave theory is an extremely complex and elegant system wor-
thy of additional investigation. Some of the later material in this book
relates directly or indirectly to Elliott's principles. Nonetheless, there
is a semiserious caveat involved when deciphering the results of
Elliott wave analysis: "Place 12 Elliotticians in different rooms with the
same financial bar chart and you will get 12 different interpretations."

Chapter **14**
Gartley Patterns

H. M. GARTLEY

Born in 1899, Harold McKinley Gartley grew up in Newark, NJ. He attended New York University, where he received a bachelor's degree in commercial science and a master's degree in business administration. He began working on Wall Street in 1922. Over the years, he was a broker, a security analyst, and a financial advisor. In addition, he gave lecture tours and private courses on the stock market that were attended by many of the prominent people of Wall Street. Gartley was one of the founders and an active member of the New York Society of Security Analysts. He also founded the Wall Street Forum for younger analysts. From 1947 on, he worked in the field of financial and shareholder public relations. In his later years, he was chairman of his own financial public relations firm until he retired in 1969.

Gartley wrote many articles on the stock market, but his best work is considered to be his book, *Profits in the Stock Market*, which was published in 1935 by Contemporary Traders and Analysts. Of special interest to many traders is his chapter entitled, "Volume of Trading." Gartley is said to have done more work on volume than anyone else. Unfortunately, Gartley's idea of "scientific" study was somewhat primitive as measured against today's standards. His approach was more rational intuitive than statistical.

GARTLEY PATTERN

The most important four-wave price formation originally analyzed by Gartley is shown in Figure 14-1.

The Gartley pattern outlined in his book did not discuss specific Fibonacci retracements. These ratios were assigned later by his supporters (primarily Scott Carney and Bryce Gilmore at Harmonic Traders), who attached very specific numeric values to the height of each of the diagonals in the Gartley pattern. The preceding pattern requires the following ratios:

$$BC = DE$$
$$BC = 0.618AB$$
$$BE = 0.786AB$$

If all three of these constraints are satisfied, then the pattern is believed to be a valid reversal.

POTENTIAL REVERSAL ZONE

The purpose of Figure 14-1 is to determine if the most recent price has entered the *potential reversal zone*. If the ratio constraints have been satisfied precisely, Gartley analysts believe that a valid reversal is in progress when the zone is penetrated.

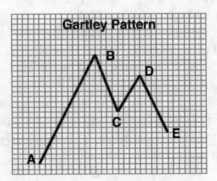

Figure 14-1   Gartley Pattern.

BUTTERFLY PATTERN

The height ratios in the butterfly pattern shown in Figure 14-2 are credited to Bryce Gilmore of Harmonic Traders.

This pattern also can have either of two different Fibonacci ratios for the fourth wave:

$$BC = 0.786\,AB$$
$$BC = 1.27\,DE$$

or

$$BC = 0.786\,AB$$
$$BC = 1.618\,DE$$

BAT PATTERN

The bat pattern shown in Figure 14-3 was discovered by Scott Carney at Harmonic Traders in 2001.

This four-wave pattern may have either of two possible ratios for the second wave:

$$BC = 0.382\,AB$$
$$DE = 1.27\,BC$$

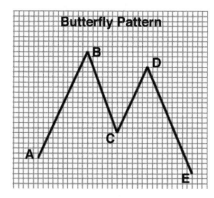

Figure 14-2 Butterfly Pattern.

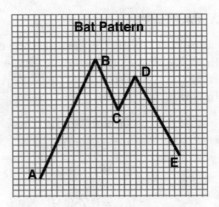

Figure 14-3 Bat Pattern.

or

$$BC = .50\,AB$$
$$DE = 1.27\,BC$$

CRAB PATTERN

The crab pattern is another discovery of Scott Carney in 2000 (Figure 14-4).

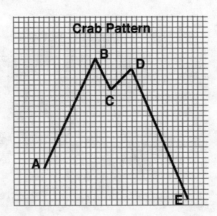

Figure 14-4 Crab Pattern.

This pattern also has two variations for the height ratio for the second wave:

$$BC = 0.618AB$$
$$CD = 1.618AB$$

or

$$BC = 0.382AB$$
$$CD = 1.618AB$$

OBSERVATIONS

It is quite clear that the Gartley studies have focused on a specific Elliott pattern (the intersection between a five-wave motive cycle and a three-wave corrective cycle), analyzed them in extreme depth, and calculated the resulting outcomes. Traders can obtain additional information on Gartley patterns at www.harmonic-traders.com.

Chapter **15**
Goodman Swing Count System

CHARLES B. GOODMAN

For nearly three decades, Charles B. Goodman was one of Denver's most successful futures traders. The principles of the Goodman swing count system were set forth informally in a series of annotated commodity charts from the late 1940s to the early 1970s.

These trading studies were simply titled, "My System," and were never published during Goodman's life time (he died in 1984). In the early 2000s, Goodman's student and protégé, Michael D. Archer, decrypted and compiled Goodman's works into a book entitled, *Forex Charting Companion* (Wiley, 2005).

The Goodman swing count system (GSCS) is based on *ordinal principles* (refers to measurement without specific values) and *cardinal principles* (refers to measurement with specific values). The system provides a fresh and penetrating insight into the examination of wave theory.

ORDINAL PRINCIPLES

1. The Measured Move

The cornerstone of the GSCS is the *50 percent retracement and measured move rule* (Figure 15-1).

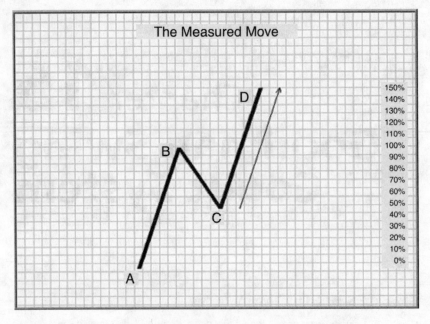

Figure 15-1 Fifty Percent Retracement and Measured Move.

The first systematic description of this rule was given in Burton Pugh's *The Great Wheat Secret* (originally published in 1933). In 1973, Charles L. Lindsay published *Trident (Trident Publishers)*. This book did much to quantify and describe the rule mathematically. Another important text in this field is *The Trading Rule That Can Make You Rich*, by Edward L. Dobson (Traders Press, 1978).

2. Congestion Phase

In 1975, a well-known Chicago grain floor trader, Eugene Nofri, published *The Congestion Phase System (Success Publishing)*. This small but power-packed volume detailed a short-term trading method using simple but effective congestion phases (Figure 15-2).

Goodman also felt that Earl Hadady's work on contrary opinion was a natural "fit," especially because the GCSC support and resistance points seldom lie where anyone else thinks they should.

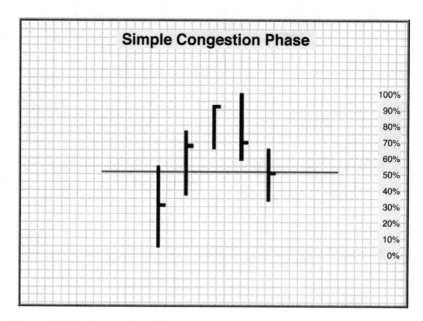

Figure 15-2 Congestion Phase.

3. Equilibrium of Buyers and Sellers

The logic of the rule is quite simple. At a 50 percent retracement, both buyers and sellers of the previous trend (up or down) are in balance. Half of each holds profits, and half of each holds losses (Figure 15-3).

The equilibrium is a tenuous one. The distribution of buyers and sellers over the initial price trend, or *swing*, is obviously not perfectly even. Some buyers hold more contracts than other buyers. They also have different propensities for taking profits or losses. Nor does the equilibrium account for the buyers and sellers who have entered the market before the initial swing or during the reaction swing. Not all the buyers and sellers from the original swing may be in the market any longer.

Remarkably, the GCSC eventually takes all of this into account, especially the buyers and sellers at other price swing levels, called *matrices*.

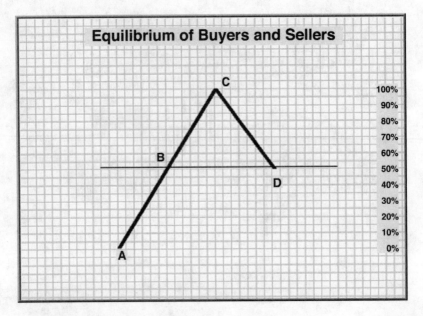

Figure 15-3   Market Tug of War.

Nevertheless, the 50 percent retracement point is often a powerful and very real point of equilibrium and certainly a known and defined hot spot of which one should be aware. Remember that both the futures markets and the currency markets are very close to a zero-sum game. It is only commissions, pips, and slippage that keep them from being zero-sum. At the 50 percent point, it does not take much to shift the balance of power for that particular swing matrix.

The rule also states that the final (third) swing of the move—back in the direction of the initial swing—will equal the value of the initial swing. The logic of this idea, called the *measured move*, is seen in Figure 15-4.

4. The Markets Are Recursive

As we have suggested previously, to examples of the rule occur at all price levels or matrices, and many are being worked simultaneously in any given ongoing market (Figure 15-5).

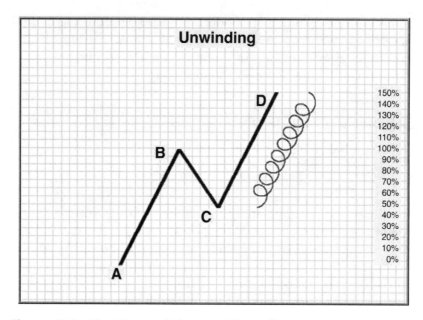

Figure 15-4 The Measured Move and Unwinding.

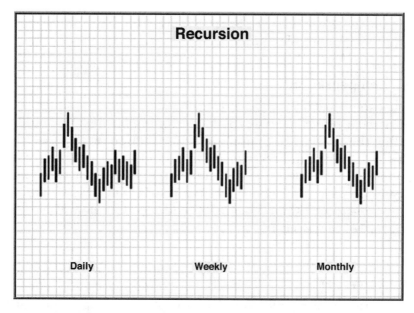

Figure 15-5 The Markets Are Recursive.

This is a critical point. In modern terminology, it would be said that price movements are *recursive*. Simply stated, this means that without labeling, you cannot really tell the difference between a 10-minute chart and a daily or weekly chart.

CARDINAL PRINCIPLES

The GSCS has six cardinal principles.

1. Price Surge

Goodman realized both the possibilities for a reversal (as in the case of the completed measured move) and a price surge. A price surge would be the equivalent to the sellers (in an uptrend) and the buyers (in a downtrend) winning the tug of war within a matrix. In price action, this means that prices would fall or rise to at least the beginning point of the initial swing.

2. Multiple-Level Matrices

Goodman discovered the implications of the rule occurring simultaneously at all price levels. This is equivalent to the fractal property in other wave systems.

3. Compensation

The extent that a price swing overshoots or undershoots its ideal 50 percent retracement will be "made up" on the next price swing within the matrix. For example, if prices fall by only 40 percent of the initial trend and reverse, the measured move actually will be either 90 or 110 percent of the measured move point and value of the primary (initial) swing in the matrix. The 10 percent difference—the GCSC holds—*must* be made up eventually. This is the concept of *compensation*.

4. Carryover

Furthermore, if the difference is not fully made up in the final price swing of a matrix, the cumulative "miss" value will carry over through each subsequent price matrix until it does. This is the concept of *carryover*. A carryover table is used to add and subtract cumulative carryover values until they cancel.

5. Cancellation

When no carryover remains, the price matrix is said to have cleared or canceled. This is the GCSC concept of *cancellation*. It is critical to finding GCSC support and resistance points and other chart hot spots where something much less than random is likely to occur.

6. Intersections

The importance of a hot spot in relationship to its likelihood of being an important point of support or resistance or reversal or continuation increases when two or more price matrices cancel at the same price or in the same price area. This is the key concept of *intersection*. There is no analogous concept in Elliott wave theory, the most common competitor to the GSCS. Intersection makes the GSCS much more objective and testable than other swing systems.

CAVEAT

All new systems almost always possess a few unresolved quirks and areas of uncertainty. Nonetheless, the GSCS offers tremendous potential for dedicated traders who wish to pursue its intricacies and do the necessary testing. This chapter is simply a summary of some of the salient features. Michael D. Archer offers comprehensive lectures on the GSCS at www.fxpraxis.com.

PART 5
Two-Wave Cycles

Chapter **16**
Properties of Two-Wave Cycles

OVERVIEW

Earlier we defined a *wave* as single diagonal line representing the slope between two price extremes and a *cycle* as a series of two or more waves. Our analysis logically begins with the smallest cycle possible, two consecutive waves. The criterion for comparing two-wave cycles is the ratio of the heights between adjacent waves. The three obvious conditions are therefore *greater than, equal to,* and *less than* (Figures 16-1 through 16-3).

Each of these diagrams has two cycles. The cycles on the left are referred to as *bull cycles,* and the cycles on the right are called *bear*

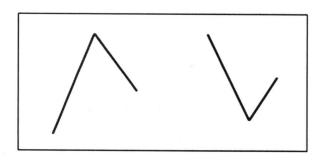

Figure 16-1   Wave 1 > Wave 2.

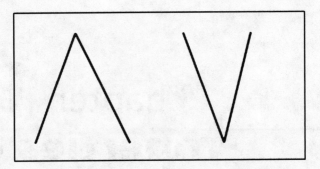

Figure 16-2   Wave 1 = Wave 2.

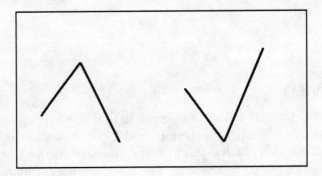

Figure 16-3   Wave 1 < Wave 2.

cycles. The direction of the first wave in a cycle determines the use of bull/bear nomenclature throughout this book.

FREQUENCIES

In Table 16-1, the two-wave relationship frequencies are expressed as percentages for several minimum reversal amounts.

Table 16-1   Two-Wave Relationship Frequencies

No.	Relationship	5-Pip	10-Pip	15-Pip	20-Pip	25-Pip	30-Pip	35-Pip
1	Wave 1 > wave 2	33.34	42.86	47.46	48.47	48.47	48.47	47.85
2	Wave 1 = wave 2	33.39	16.20	5.91	3.47	1.66	1.16	1.12
3	Wave 1 < wave 2	33.26	40.93	46.63	48.06	49.89	49.57	51.03

It is assumed that relationships 1 and 3 will approximate each other automatically when a large sample is analyzed. This table is included here simply to display the decreasing values for the equality relationship as the minimum reversal amount increases. For example, using a 20-pip minimum reversal amount, there is only 3.5 percent likelihood that two adjacent waves will be equal in height.

BASIC MODEL

The first test is to determine if the heights of any two consecutive waves provide sufficient data to forecast the height of the subsequent wave accurately. This uses the generic linear autoregressive model, namely,

$$Z_{t+1} = AZ_{t-1} + BZ_t + \varepsilon_t$$

and more specifically,

$$\text{Wave } 3 = A \times \text{wave } 1 + B \times \text{wave } 2$$

Where A = first partial coefficient of regression
B = second partial coefficient of regression
ε = error factor

INITIAL TEST

The first step is to convert the 29 million + streaming quotes in our EURUSD 2005 database into swing data using various minimum reversal amounts. By applying an ordinary least squares (OLS) regression to the swing data, the results shown in Table 16-2 were obtained.

The column headers are defined as follows:

Rev Amt—the minimum reversal amount used in the swing reversal algorithm

No. Waves—the number of diagonals created by the swing algorithm

Table 16-2 Autoregressive Partial Coefficients

Rev Amt	No. Waves	Mean Ratio	A	B	SEE	COR
5	912,385	1.0338	0.2674	0.7573	0.2683	26.93
10	61,961	1.0626	0.3452	0.6960	0.3792	34.12
15	11,632	1.1202	0.3396	0.7399	0.5485	33.74
20	4,788	1.1519	0.3228	0.7797	0.6276	32.85
25	2,656	1.1619	0.2933	0.8199	0.6550	30.19
30	1,640	1.7443	0.3170	0.8009	0.6802	32.27
35	1,164	1.1742	0.3330	0.7805	0.6674	35.40
40	850	1.1774	0.2958	0.8290	0.7220	29.35
45	668	1.1731	0.3189	0.7972	0.6896	32.96
50	538	1.1759	0.3180	0.7984	0.6906	34.12

Mean Ratio—the average ratio of the third (extrapolated) wave divided by the second wave

A—the partial regression coefficient for the first wave
B—the partial regression coefficient for the second wave

SEE—standard error of the estimate

COR—the coefficient of regression expressed as a percentage

INTERPRETATION

Statistically, the results in Table 16-2 are not surprising, as defined by the crucial final column, the coefficient of correlation. An average value of 31 percent indicates that less than one-third the height of the third wave can be attributed directly to the heights of the two previous waves. The generic model above therefore is inadequate as a valid third-wave forecaster.

Chapter **17**
Enhancing the Forecast

OVERVIEW

The basic autoregressive model discussed in Chapter 16 is too generic to serve a useful purpose under certain circumstances. Therefore, some simple constraints must be imposed on the relationship between the first and second waves. Our new approach is to create three separate tests using the following height relationships:

> *Test A:* Height of wave 2 less than one-third the height of wave 1

> *Test B:* Height of wave 2 greater than one-third the height of wave 1 and less than two-thirds the height of wave 1

> *Test C:* Height of wave 2 greater than two-thirds the height of wave 1 and less than the height of wave 1

FIRST-TERCILE TESTING

In Tables 17-1 to 17-3, the values in the "Mean Ratio" column are calculated as the height of wave 3 divided by the height of wave 1.

Table 17-1   First-Tercile Regression Coefficients

Rev Amt	No. Waves	Mean Ratio	A	B	SEE	COR
5	376	0.3465	0.1164	0.8292	0.1226	87.74
10	208	0.4141	0.0291	1.3832	0.1763	82.37
15	159	0.4213	0.0493	1.3265	0.1861	81.39
20	108	0.4221	0.1470	0.9952	0.1709	82.91
25	68	0.4051	−0.1041	1.8477	0.2101	78.99

Table 17-2   Second-Tercile Regression Coefficients

Rev Amt	No. Waves	Mean Ratio	A	B	SEE	COR
5	46,021	0.6574	0.0422	1.0846	0.1699	83.01
10	5,602	0.6829	0.1474	0.9843	0.2630	73.70
15	1,904	0.7201	0.0828	1.2051	0.3352	66.48
20	865	0.7365	−0.0196	1.4619	0.3847	61.53
25	507	0.7304	−0.0194	1.4538	0.3723	62.77

Table 17-3   Third-Tercile Regression Coefficients

Rev Amt	No. Waves	Mean Ratio	A	B	SEE	COR
5	257,834	0.8769	0.3523	0.6483	0.2209	77.91
10	20,747	0.9635	0.2717	0.8315	0.3279	67.21
15	3,457	1.0465	0.4256	0.7503	0.4935	50.65
20	1,347	1.0723	0.5493	0.6341	0.5405	45.95
25	711	1.1161	0.4020	0.8634	0.6140	38.60

USE

First, we observe that partitioning the sample data into three equal divisions has greatly enhanced the coefficient of correlation, particularly in the first tercile. To illustrate that these tables can be put to practical use, we include the following example.

Assume that we employed a 10-pip minimum reversal amount to create the swing data. Also assume that the last two known waves in the swing data are 19 and 12 pips, respectively. Since 12 is greater than one-third of 19 and less than two-thirds of 19, we use the second-tercile table to calculate the height of the next wave. We use the basic model

$$\text{Wave } 3 = A \times \text{wave } 1 + B \times \text{wave } 2$$

and substitute our known wave heights:

$$\text{Wave } 3 = A \times 19 \text{ pips} + B \times 12 \text{ pips}$$

Next, we replace A and B with the corresponding values in the second-tercile table:

$$\text{Wave } 3 = 0.1474 \times 19 \text{ pips} + 0.9843 \times 12 \text{ pips}$$

Then we multiply the coefficients:

$$\text{Wave } 3 = 2.8006 + 11.8116$$

and add the two products:

$$\text{Wave } 3 = 14.6122$$

Thus there is a 74 percent likelihood (the coefficient of correlation) that the next wave will be 15 pips in height (Figure 17-1).

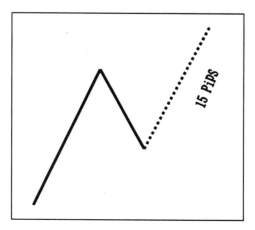

Figure 17-1 Third-Wave Forecast.

There is a quicker (though less accurate) method to calculate the height of the next wave. Simply multiply the height of the first wave by the corresponding mean ratio in the table:

$$\text{Wave } 3 = \text{wave } 1 \times \text{mean ratio}$$
$$\text{Wave } 3 = 19 \text{ pips} \times 0.6829$$
$$\text{Wave } 3 = 13 \text{ pips}$$

The analytical approach illustrated in this chapter may appear somewhat simplistic to some traders. However, it is necessary in order to lay down a foundation for more advanced forms of ratio analysis and autoregression used in later chapters.

PART 6
Three-Wave Cycles

Chapter 18
Basic Types of Three-Wave Cycles

OVERVIEW

As in Chapter 17, the criterion for identifying a basic three-wave cycle is the relationship between the heights of the individual waves using the three comparison operators:

> greater than

= equal to

< less than

These operators define nine unique bull cycles and nine unique bear cycles. If the first wave in any cycle is upward, then the entire cycle is referred to as a *bull cycle*. If the first wave in any cycle is downward, then the entire cycle is called a *bear cycle*. Each three-wave cycle is identified by a one-letter label (ID). Bull cycles use the uppercase letters "A" through "I," whereas bear cycles are designated by the lowercase letters "a" through "i."

IMPULSE CYCLE (ID = A)

The single most important three-wave cycle is called an *impulse cycle*, a term borrowed from the Elliott wave principle. This pattern defines a clear and consistent trend in either price direction. The cycle begins with a price surge followed by a retracement wave whose height is less than the height of the initial surge wave. The height of the final wave must exceed the height of the retracement wave (Figure 18-1).

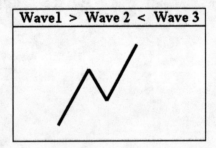

Figure 18-1   Impulse Cycle.

RECTANGLE (ID = B)

The second three-wave cycle occurs less frequently than the impulse cycle because the heights of all three waves must be the same. The rectangle formation represents a horizontal price movement, also called *lateral congestion* (Figure 18-2).

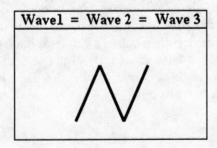

Figure 18-2   Rectangle.

CONTRACTING DESCENDING TRIANGLE (ID = C)

This cycle is identified as two waves of the same height followed by one wave whose height is less than either of its two predecessor waves (Figure 18-3).

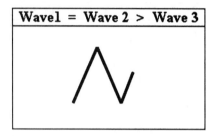

Figure 18-3 Contracting Descending Triangle.

CONTRACTING ASCENDING TRIANGLE (ID = D)

This cycle is identified as a price-surge wave followed by two waves whose heights are equal to or less than the height of the initial wave (Figure 18-4).

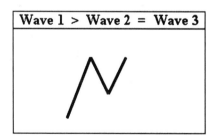

Figure 18-4 Contracting Ascending Triangle.

CONTRACTING SYMMETRICAL TRIANGLE (ID = E)

This cycle is identified as an initial price-surge wave followed by two waves whose heights are less than the immediate predecessor wave (Figure 18-5).

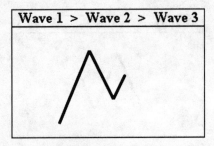

Figure 18-5 Contracting Symmetrical Triangle.

EXPANDING ASCENDING TRIANGLE (ID = F)

This cycle is identified as two waves whose heights are equal followed by a final wave whose height is greater than either of its predecessor waves (Figure 18-6).

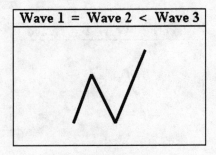

Figure 18-6 Expanding Ascending Triangle.

EXPANDING DESCENDING TRIANGLE (ID = G)

This cycle is identified as an initial wave whose successor waves are both greater than the initial wave but equal to each other (Figure 18-7).

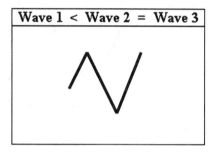

Figure 18-7 Expanding Descending Triangle.

EXPANDING SYMMETRICAL TRIANGLE (ID = H)

This cycle is identified as an initial price-surge wave followed by two waves whose heights are greater than the immediate predecessor wave (Figure 18-8).

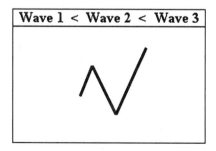

Figure 18-8 Expanding Symmetrical Triangle.

CONNECTOR (ID = I)

This cycle is so named because it links two impulse cycles together to create an even longer trend cycle. The height of the middle wave is always greater than the heights of either two adjacent waves (Figure 18-9).

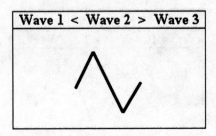

Figure 18-9   Connector.

BEAR-CYCLE CONVERSION

Each three-wave bull cycle can be converted to an equivalent bear cycle simply by rotating the cycle 180 degrees along its x axis (or in nontechnical parlance, "flipping" the cycle vertically). The height-comparison constraints remain the same, but the first wave now points downward. Four of the triangle designations become reversed, as shown in Table 18-1 (reversed names are displayed in italics).

FREQUENCIES

Table 18-2 expresses the frequencies of the three-wave cycles as percentages for several minimum reversal amounts. Bull and bear cycles have been added together.

Several interesting cycle properties are exhibited in this table. As the minimum reversal amount for the swing algorithm increases, two seemingly opposite phenomena occur:

1. The frequencies of the impulse cycles, both symmetrical triangles, and the connector cycles also increase.

2. The frequencies of the rectangles, both ascending triangles, and both descending triangles decrease.

Table 18-1   Bear-Cycle Conversions

No.	Bull Name	ID	Bear Name	ID
1	Impulse	A	Impulse	a
2	Rectangle	B	Rectangle	b
3	Contracting Descending Triangle	C	*Contracting Ascending Triangle*	c
4	Contracting Ascending Triangle	D	*Contracting Descending Triangle*	d
5	Contracting Symmetrical Triangle	E	Contracting Symmetrical Triangle	e
6	Expanding Ascending Triangle	F	*Expanding Descending Triangle*	f
7	Expanding Descending Triangle	G	*Expanding Ascending Triangle*	g
8	Expanding Symmetrical Triangle	H	Expanding Symmetrical Triangle	h
9	Connector	I	Connector	i

The reason for this is quite simple: The cycles that decrease in frequency all have equality relationships between the heights of two or more waves in those cycles. Naturally, as the heights of two adjacent waves increase, there is less likelihood that they will be the same magnitude because the y-axis resolution is growing more and more graduated. Mathematically, this is analogous to the outcome of throwing different numbers of dice. Tossing two dice at

Table 18-2   Three-Wave-Cycle Frequencies

ID	Cycle Name	5-Pip	10-Pip	15-Pip	20-Pip	25-Pip	30-Pip	35-Pip
A	Impulse	13.3	22.9	29.5	30.9	31.8	32.5	33.7
B	Rectangle	12.8	3.7	0.6	0.2	0.0	0.1	0.0
C	Con Desc Triangle	7.6	4.2	1.7	0.8	0.5	0.4	0.3
D	Con Asc Triangle	13.1	8.6	3.5	2.2	1.5	0.7	0.7
E	Con Sym Triangle	6.9	11.3	14.5	15.4	15.7	16.1	13.5
F	Exp Asc Triangle	13.0	8.3	3.6	2.4	1.2	0.7	0.8
G	Exp Desc Triangle	7.5	3.9	1.8	1.1	0.6	0.4	0.4
H	Exp Sym Triangle	6.9	9.7	13.6	14.7	16.9	16.2	16.6
I	Connector	18.9	27.3	31.6	32.2	32.3	32.9	34.0

one time renders 36 possibilities. Throwing four dice at the same time generates 1,296 possibilities (thus greater gradation).

One more curiosity can be observed in Table 18-2. In all the different minimum reversal amounts, the connector cycle always ranked at the top of the list in frequency count, even surpassing the impulse cycle that we originally expected to head the list. This fact will be useful in later studies.

Chapter **19**
Forecasting the Third Wave

FORECASTING WAVE RELATIONSHIPS

Table 18-1 in the preceding chapter not only exhibits the frequency data for three-wave cycles but also provides sufficient information to forecast the logical length of the third wave when only the first two waves are known. By *logical length*, we mean the result of the comparative ratio length using the logical operators $>$, $=$, and $<$.

PRACTICAL EXAMPLE

For example, assume that the final two waves in the swing data form the pattern shown in Figure 19-1.

We automatically know that there are three possible continuations once the next wave is known: an impulse cycle, a contracting ascending triangle and a contracting symmetrical triangle (Figure 19-2).

From Table 18-1, we obtain the percentages for a 35-pip reversal amount for the possible continuations, as shown in Table 19-1.

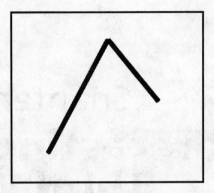

Figure 19-1   Two-Wave Pattern (Wave 1 > Wave 2).

The next step is to sum the percentages in Table 19-1 and divide that sum into each value (Table 19-2):

$$33.7 + 0.7 + 13.5 = 48.9$$

Given the two-wave pattern in Figure 19-1, this means that when using a 35-pip swing reversal amount, there is a 69 percent likelihood that the next wave in the swing data will surpass the top of wave 1 and become a "full" three-wave impulse cycle.

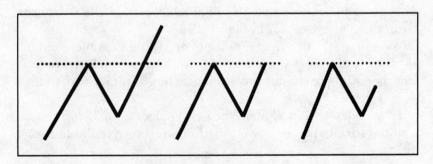

Figure 19-2   Possible Third-Wave Continuations.

Table 19-1   Raw Percentages

Cycle Name	Percent
Impulse	33.7
Contracting ascending triangle	0.7
Contracting symmetrical triangle	13.5

Table 19-2   Adjusted Percentages

Cycle Name	Percent
Impulse	69.0
Contracting ascending triangle	1.4
Contracting symmetrical triangle	27.6

CAVEAT

Although a 69 percent probability is a rather respectable trigger value when considering a possible market-entry order, the disadvantage is that the standard deviation is very high when basing the forecast solely on the two preceding wave heights. However, methods are presented in later chapters to lower the standard deviation and improve the level of confidence. (Such methods involve basing the forecast on more than just two preceding waves.)

PART 7
Four-Wave Cycles

Chapter **20**
Names of Multiwave Cycles

OVERVIEW

In earlier chapters we indicated that the basic cycle consists of three consecutive waves and is identifiable by a single unique letter between "A" and "I" or "a" and "i" using the three logical operators $>$, $=$, and $<$. In this chapter we will introduce a method for naming cycles with four or more waves.

OVERLAPPING WAVES

When analyzing cycles consisting of more than three waves, we have devised a naming convention that uses an overlapping-wave technique (Figure 20-1).

For example, the four-wave cycle in this figure can be decomposed into the two overlapping three-wave cycles, as shown in Figure 20-2.

Wave 2–3 on the left aligns perfectly with the wave 2–3 on the right. The same is true for the waves 3–4 on the left and the right. The three-wave cycle on the left is a bull impulse cycle

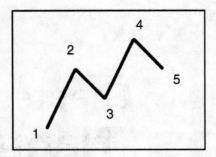

Figure 20-1 Basic Four-Wave Cycle.

(designated "A"), whereas the three-wave cycle on the right is a bear connector cycle (designated "i"). Thus, in our naming scheme, the four-wave cycle in Figure 20-1 is labeled "Ai."

This naming convention can be extended indefinitely by adding a new letter to the current cycle name each time a new wave is appended. In the next example (Figure 20-3), a six-wave cycle is "decomposed" and labeled.

The individual three-wave components are listed in Table 20-1.

Thus the six-wave cycle in Figure 20-3 is identified as an "AiFa" cycle pattern.

Note that the first and second waves of the rightmost cycle are overlaid exactly on the second and third waves in the leftmost cycle. Both the heights (*y* axis) and the widths (*x* axis) of the two shared waves must align perfectly to form a new wave cycle.

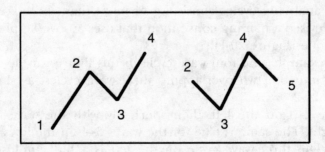

Figure 20-2 Components of a Four-Wave Cycle.

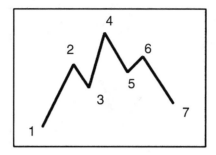

Figure 20-3   Six-Wave Cycle.

NAMING CONVENTION

It is obvious that the four-wave cycle in Figure 20-1 is actually the concatenation (or partial merging) of a three-wave bull impulse cycle and a three-wave bear connector cycle. Our labeling convention to identify the new four-wave cycle is "Ai."

Because of the constraints imposed by the three logical operators ($>$, $=$, and $<$) between adjacent waves, each three-wave cycle may be merged only with three of the nine possible three-wave cycles. For example, the bull impulse cycle can only be overlapped with a bear connector, a bear expanding ascending triangle, or a bear expanding symmetrical triangle. These are the three cycles in which the height of the second wave is always greater than the height of the first wave.

To further clarify the naming convention for four-wave cycles, we present one more example (Figure 20-4).

Table 20-1   Component Waves

Components	Cycle Name	Cycle ID
1–2–3–4	Bull impulse	A
2–3–4–5	Bear connector	i
3–4–5–6	Bull contracting symmetrical triangle	F
4–5–6–7	Bear impulse	a

Figure 20-4 Four-Wave Bear Cycle.

The three waves on the left in Figure 20-4 form a bear contracting symmetrical triangle, whereas the three waves on the right form a bull impulse cycle. Thus the four-wave cycle in Figure 20-4 is designated as "eA."

Chapter **21**
Properties of Four-Wave Cycles

OVERVIEW

Using the same logical height relationship that was applied to three-wave cycles, there are 27 possible four-wave patterns $(3 \times 3 \times 3 = 27)$.

FREQUENCIES

Table 21-1 is a frequency table that is sorted in descending order by 25-pip reversal amount.

Interesting to note in this table is the sharp decline in frequency beginning with the cycle "FI." All cycles above "FI" only use the "greater than" or the "less than" relationship.

FORECASTING THE FOURTH WAVE

Given any three-wave cycle, we can estimate the relationship between the third and fourth waves using Table 21-2.

In the next example (Figure 21-1), we will assume that a 15-pip swing reversal amount was used to create the swing data being scrutinized and that the last three-wave cycle was a bull connector cycle.

Table 21-1 Four-Wave Cycles Sorted by
25-Pip Reversal

Cycle	5-Pip	15-Pip	25-Pip
IA	6.84	18.16	19.73
AI	6.76	18.69	18.93
HI	5.07	10.39	12.59
AH	3.47	9.46	12.28
IE	5.00	10.89	11.87
EA	3.45	10.08	11.64
HH	0.82	2.87	4.27
EE	0.85	3.23	3.78
FI	7.03	2.20	0.79
DF	6.54	2.41	0.72
ID	7.01	2.22	0.72
AG	3.11	1.33	0.57
GF	1.52	0.81	0.42
CA	3.05	1.24	0.42
FH	2.60	1.24	0.38
ED	2.62	1.16	0.26
GC	4.05	0.85	0.23
DC	1.53	0.74	0.23
HG	1.01	0.32	0.08
CE	1.07	0.34	0.04
DB	5.02	0.37	0.04
BF	4.97	0.35	0.04
GB	1.94	0.11	0.00
BB	5.84	0.14	0.00
BC	1.99	0.13	0.00
CD	3.46	0.14	0.00
FG	3.39	0.13	0.00

The three possible continuations for the overlapping cycle are
a contracting symmetrical bear cycle (ID = "e"), a contracting
descending bear cycle (ID = "d"), and a bear connector cycle
(ID = "i") (Figure 21-2).

From Table 21-2, we find the frequencies shown in Table 21-3
for the connector cycle.

Thus there is over a 65 percent likelihood that the fourth wave
will touch or descend below the lowest point in the third wave
when using a 15-pip reversal amount.

Table 21-2 Four-Wave Cycle Percentages Sorted by Cycle ID

Cycle	5-Pips	15-Pips	25-Pips
AG	3.11	1.33	0.57
AH	3.47	9.46	12.28
AI	6.76	18.69	18.93
BB	5.84	0.14	0.00
BC	1.99	0.13	0.00
BF	4.97	0.35	0.04
CA	3.05	1.24	0.42
CD	3.46	0.14	0.00
CE	1.07	0.34	0.04
DB	5.02	0.37	0.04
DC	1.53	0.74	0.23
DF	6.54	2.41	0.72
EA	3.45	10.08	11.64
ED	2.62	1.16	0.26
EE	0.85	3.23	3.78
FG	3.39	0.13	0.00
FH	2.60	1.24	0.38
FI	7.03	2.20	0.79
GB	1.94	0.11	0.00
GC	4.05	0.85	0.23
GF	1.52	0.81	0.42
HG	1.01	0.32	0.08
HH	0.82	2.87	4.27
HI	5.0780	10.39	12.59
IA	6.84	18.16	19.73
ID	7.01	2.22	0.72
IE	5.00	10.89	11.87

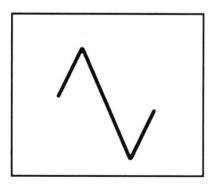

Figure 21-1 Three-Wave Bull Connector Cycle.

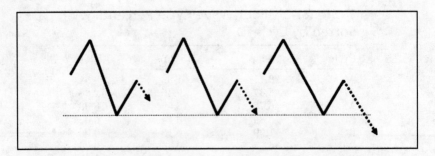

Figure 21-2   Possible Fourth-Wave Continuations.

Table 21-3   Connector Cycle Percentages

Cycle ID	Raw Percent	Adjusted Percent
IA	18.16	58.08
ID	2.22	7.10
IE	10.89	34.82

PART 8
Five-Wave Cycles

Chapter **22**
Properties of Five-Wave Cycles

PRUNING

As the minimum reversal amount is increased, five of the nine basic three-wave cycles decrease in frequency of occurrence owing to the equality relationship. We will arbitrarily refer to these cycles as *secondary* cycles, indicating that their low frequency equates to less importance. Specifically, these cycles are listed in Table 22-1.

The four remaining cycle types will be referred to as *primary* cycles because their greater frequency of occurrence implies greater importance. They are listed in Table 22-2.

The purpose for making this distinction is to lessen the number of cycle permutations that will occur when examining cycles composed of more than four waves. Using the overlapping methodology to name all five-wave cycles, there are 81 possibilities ($9 \times 3 \times 3 = 81$).

However, by removing all the secondary cycles, this number is reduced significantly to only 16 permutations ($4 \times 2 \times 2 = 16$). In

Table 22-1 Secondary Cycle Types

Cycle ID	Cycle Name
B	Rectangle
C	Contracting descending triangle
D	Contracting ascending triangle
F	Expanding ascending triangle
G	Expanding descending triangle

other words, we are dropping the "equals" condition from the height ratio criteria. We are now concerned only with "greater than" or "less than" height ratios. This form of pruning is justified mathematically because it keeps the data and the results more manageable.

FREQUENCIES

In Table 22-3, cycles are sorted in descending order of the fourth column.

There is no surprise that the trending cycles "IAI" and "AIA" lead the list. It is interesting to note, though, that the 5- and 15-pip reversal amounts do not exactly match the order of the 25-pip reversal amount.

Table 22-2 Primary Cycle Types

Cycle ID	Cycle Name
A	Impulse
E	Contracting symmetrical triangle
H	Expanding symmetrical triangle
I	Connector

Table 22-3 Five-Wave Cycles Sorted by 25-Pip Reversal Amount

Cycle ID	5-Pips	15-Pips	25-Pips
IAI	15.92	14.91	13.14
AIA	11.78	14.40	12.70
AHI	10.92	8.97	9.46
IEA	10.77	9.43	9.10
HIA	6.84	7.01	7.84
IAH	7.52	7.11	7.64
AIE	6.53	7.59	7.12
EAI	7.25	7.86	6.79
EAH	4.12	4.17	5.38
HIE	8.05	5.26	5.30
HHI	2.91	3.01	3.72
AHH	1.93	2.70	3.60
IEE	2.86	3.22	3.40
EEA	1.91	3.06	3.32
HHH	0.30	0.55	0.85
EEE	0.39	0.73	0.65

Chapter **23**
Forecasting the Fifth Wave

OVERVIEW

Table 23-1 is sorted by cycle ID and provides the information necessary to calculate probabilities for the binary relationships "greater than" and "less than" for height ratios.

EXTENDED IMPULSE CYCLE

In our naming convention, we define a four-wave extended impulse cycle as "Ai" because it has the potential to become a five-wave Elliot impulse cycle, as shown in Figure 23-1.

Using a 15-pip reversal amount and referring to Table 23-1, we can calculate the likelihood that a full five-wave bull Elliott impulse cycle ("AiA") will come to fruition:

$$AiA = 14.40$$
$$AiE = 7.59$$
$$\text{Probability of AiA} = 100 \times 14.40 / (14.40 + 7.59)$$
$$\text{Probability of AiA} = 65.5 \text{ percent}$$

This 66 percent likelihood gives some credibility to the ancient maxim, "A trend continues until it ends."

Table 23-1   Five-Wave Cycle Frequencies Sorted by Cycle ID

Cycle ID	5-Pips	15-Pips	25-Pips
AHH	1.93	2.70	3.60
AHI	10.92	8.97	9.46
AIA	11.78	14.40	12.70
AIE	6.53	7.59	7.12
EAH	4.12	4.17	5.38
EAI	7.25	7.86	6.79
EEA	1.91	3.06	3.32
EEE	0.39	0.73	0.65
HHH	0.30	0.55	0.85
HHI	2.91	3.01	3.72
HIA	6.84	7.01	7.84
HIE	8.05	5.26	5.30
IAH	7.52	7.11	7.64
IAI	15.92	14.91	13.14
IEA	10.77	9.43	9.10
IEE	2.86	3.22	3.40

POTENTIAL HEAD AND SHOULDERS

Head and shoulders patterns represent trend reversals and, as such, should be examined closely. The head and shoulders pattern that we will analyze has the critical descending neckline (cycle ID = "Ah"), as shown in Figure 23-2.

The first indication that the highest point in the third wave is in fact a major reversal point is that the fifth wave does not exceed this point. Thus we need to calculate the probability that the cycle

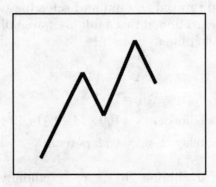

Figure 23-1   Potential Five-Wave Elliott Impulse Cycle.

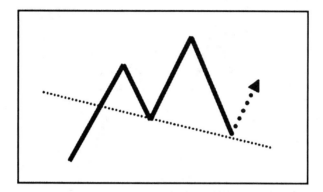

Figure 23-2 Head and Shoulders with Descending Neckline.

"AhI" will occur. Again, refer to Table 23-1, this time using a 5-pip reversal amount.

$$AhI = 10.92$$
$$AhH = 1.93$$
$$\text{Probability of AhI} = 100 \times 10.92/(10.92 + 1.93)$$
$$\text{Probability of AhI} = 85.0 \text{ percent}$$

This is a very promising result. There is an 85 percent likelihood that the fifth wave will be the beginning of a downward trend. Note the relation between this pattern and the previous one, the extended impulse cycle, where the height of the fourth wave is the only difference. The extended impulse cycle has the potential to be a head and shoulders pattern with an ascending neckline, but the probability is far less.

EXTENDED CONTRACTING TRIANGLE

From classical pattern-recognition theory, we recall that triangles normally are considered to be continuation harbingers. This may be an optimistic appraisal that we feel requires testing. We will examine the bull contracting symmetrical triangle (cycle ID = "Ee") using a 25-pip reversal amount, as shown in Figure 23-3.

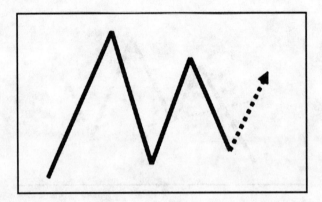

Figure 23-3 Extended Contracting Symmetrical Triangle.

Our premise is that the trend of the first wave is the current overall trend. Therefore, we want to calculate the likelihood that the
fifth wave will be greater than the fourth wave.

$$EeA = 3.32$$
$$EeE = 0.65$$
$$\text{Probability of } EeA = 100 \times 3.32/(3.32 + 0.65)$$
$$\text{Probability of } EeA = 83.6 \text{ percent}$$

This implies that there is an 84 percent likelihood that the existing trend prior to a double contracting symmetrical triangle will
continue. Contracting triangles harbor their own unique fascina-
tion, not unlike increasing the torque on a metal spring. Sharp
breakouts frequently follow these triangles.

EXTENDED EXPANDING TRIANGLE

Extended expanding triangles are a sign that the market is both
highly volatile and very confused. Perhaps indecisive is a better
word (Figure 23-4).

Expanding triangles are the only pattern that cannot be maintained indefinitely. In fact, in the 29 million + EURUSD database
covering the tick data for calendar year 2005, there was only one

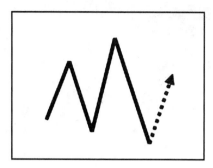

Figure 23-4 Extended Expanding Symmetrical Triangle.

occurrence of an "HhHhH" cycle, a seven-wave expanding triangle. Therefore, we will calculate the probability that the height of the fifth wave in this cycle will be less than the height of the fourth wave, thus terminating the expanding phenomenon. We will employ a 5-pip reversal amount in this example.

$$HhI = 2.91$$
$$HhH = 0.30$$
$$\text{Probability of } HhI = 100 \times 2.91/(2.91 + 0.30)$$
$$\text{Probability of } HhI = 90.7 \text{ percent}$$

This result is not surprising, merely good to know, particularly when dealing with higher swing reversal amounts. We also should note that contracting triangles theoretically can be maintained over time simply by entering a phase of zero activity where the last price lingers indefinitely (such as weekends).

This 91 percent probability represents about as close to a "sure thing" as is possible when forecasting with wave theory.

PART 9
Six-Wave Cycles

Chapter **24**
Properties of
Six-Wave Cycles

OVERVIEW

Using the three logical operators $>$, $<$, and $=$ for height-ratio comparisons of six-wave cycles generates 243 permutations ($9 \times 3 \times 3 \times 3 = 243$). By excluding the equality relationship, the number of permutations is reduced to 32 possibilities ($4 \times 2 \times 2 \times 2 = 32$).

FREQUENCIES

Table 24-1 lists six-wave cycle frequencies sorted in descending order on the fourth column.

Note the visible decrease in frequency between the second and third rows. Also again we find the extended contracting and expanding triangles at the bottom of the frequency list.

Table 24-1   Six-Wave Cycles Sorted by 25-Pip Reversal Amount

Cycle	5-Pips	15-Pips	25-Pips
AIAI	8.83	9.70	9.26
IAIA	9.17	9.33	9.07
IEAI	7.50	6.33	6.02
IAHI	7.67	5.73	5.71
AIEA	4.85	5.66	5.55
IAIE	4.91	5.36	5.27
EAIA	3.90	5.40	5.20
AHIA	4.82	4.94	5.11
HIAI	5.24	5.03	5.07
AIAH	4.15	4.94	4.95
AHIE	5.47	3.92	3.85
HIEA	5.29	3.66	3.71
IEAH	3.93	3.18	3.40
EAHI	4.06	3.22	3.36
IEEA	2.06	2.48	2.54
AHHI	2.19	2.34	2.47
EAIE	2.34	2.38	2.35
HIAH	2.42	2.08	2.21
EEAI	1.18	1.87	1.90
HHIA	1.16	1.75	1.85
AIEE	1.00	1.74	1.79
IAHH	1.35	1.61	1.71
HIEE	1.80	1.44	1.43
HHIE	1.69	1.21	1.30
EAHH	0.76	1.11	1.22
EEAH	0.83	1.13	1.16
IEEE	0.43	0.69	0.68
EEEA	0.30	0.65	0.64
HHHI	0.36	0.53	0.59
AHHH	0.24	0.47	0.53
HHHH	0.03	0.06	0.06
EEEE	0.05	0.06	0.05

Chapter **25**
Forecasting the Sixth Wave

OVERVIEW

When analyzing cycles composed of six waves, we must note that these are not just randomly connected cycles. Our overlapping wave scheme ensures that the four central three-wave cycles are tightly linked to the adjacent cycles using the logical height-ratio comparisons.

Table 25-1 lists six-wave cycles that have been sorted by cycle ID to facilitate forecasting the sixth wave.

EXTENDED IMPULSE CYCLE

Given the five-wave impulse cycle shown in Figure 25-1, we want to determine the likelihood that the sixth wave will be shorter than the fifth wave, thereby facilitating still another bull wave continuing the upward trend.

The frequencies from Table 25-1 using a 15-pip reversal amount are

$$AiAi = 9.70$$
$$AiAh = 4.94$$
$$\text{Probability of } AiAi = 100 \times 9.70/(9.70 + 4.94)$$
$$\text{Probability of } AiAi = 66.3 \text{ percent}$$

Table 25-1 Six-Wave Cycles Sorted by Cycle ID

Cycle	5-Pips	15-Pips	25-Pips
AHHH	0.24	0.47	0.53
AHHI	2.19	2.34	2.47
AHIA	4.82	4.94	5.11
AHIE	5.47	3.92	3.85
AIAH	4.15	4.94	4.95
AIAI	8.83	9.70	9.26
AIEA	4.85	5.66	5.55
AIEE	1.00	1.74	1.79
EAHH	0.76	1.11	1.22
EAHI	4.06	3.22	3.36
EAIA	3.90	5.40	5.20
EAIE	2.34	2.38	2.35
EEAH	0.83	1.13	1.16
EEAI	1.18	1.87	1.90
EEEA	0.30	0.65	0.64
EEEE	0.05	0.06	0.05
HHHH	0.03	0.06	0.06
HHHI	0.36	0.53	0.59
HHIA	1.16	1.75	1.85
HHIE	1.69	1.21	1.30
HIAH	2.42	2.08	2.21
HIAI	5.24	5.03	5.07
HIEA	5.29	3.66	3.71
HIEE	1.80	1.44	1.43
IAHH	1.35	1.61	1.71
IAHI	7.67	5.73	5.71
IAIA	9.17	9.33	9.07
IAIE	4.91	5.36	5.27
IEAH	3.93	3.18	3.40
IEAI	7.50	6.33	6.02
IEEA	2.06	2.48	2.54
IEEE	0.43	0.69	0.68

Thus there is a two out of three chance that a five-wave impulse cycle will continue trending in the same direction. This formation should be confirmed by using different swing reversal amounts.

HEAD AND SHOULDERS

A five-wave head and shoulders formation with a descending neckline is designated "AhI." We want to calculate the probability that the sixth wave will fall below the vertex of the fourth and fifth waves, thus confirming that a reversal is actually in progress (Figure 25-2).

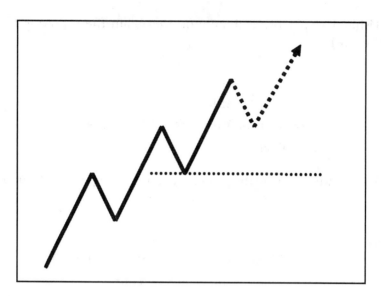

Figure 25-1 Extended Impulse Cycle.

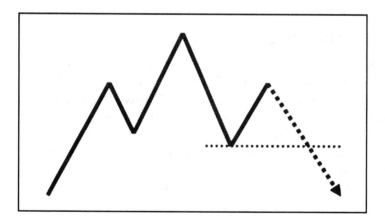

Figure 25-2 Head and Shoulders Forecast.

Using a 25-pip reversal amount, we obtain the following from Table 25-1:

$$AhIa = 5.11$$
$$AhIe = 3.85$$
$$\text{Probability of } AhIa = 100 \times 5.11/(5.11 + 3.85)$$
$$\text{Probability of } AhIe = 57.0 \text{ percent}$$

We also will calculate the probability using a 5-pip reversal amount:

$$AhIa = 4.82$$
$$AhJe = 5.47$$
$$\text{Probability of } AhIa = 100 \times 4.82/(4.82 + 5.47)$$
$$\text{Probability of } AhIe = 46.8 \text{ percent}$$

Fortunately, this inconsistency where probabilities lie on both sides of the 50 percent median when using different reversal amounts is very rare. When in doubt, stay out of the market.

CHIMERA CYCLE

In this example, we will analyze a five-wave chimera cycle so named because of its changeling properties (Figure 25-3). It starts as a contracting symmetrical triangle and ends as an expanding symmetrical triangle (cycle ID = EaH). This cycle occurs frequently during lateral congestion.

We want to test to determine if the sixth wave will drop below the vertex of the fourth and fifth waves. This time we will use a 15-pip reversal amount in Table 25-1:

$$AhIa = 4.82$$
$$AhJe = 5.47$$
$$\text{Probability of } AhIa = 100 \times 4.82/(4.82 + 5.47)$$
$$\text{Probability of } AhIe = 46.8 \text{ percent}$$

There is a 74 percent likelihood that the sixth wave will not descend below the vertex of the fourth and fifth waves.

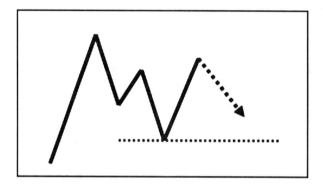

Figure 25-3 Chimera Cycle Forecast.

Chapter **26**
Double-Wave Forecasting

OVERVIEW

In previous chapters we used the height ratios of two or more waves to extrapolate the height ratio of the next single wave in the swing data. In this chapter we will illustrate examples of double-wave forecasting. The object is to determine the likelihood that a future point (the final point in the extrapolated two waves) will fall above or below the last known point in the swing data (Figure 26-1).

METHODOLOGY

To accomplish this task, we need to use the actual raw frequency counts rather than the adjusted frequency percentages. In all cases, a 15-pip minimum reversal amount will be employed.

First, we will examine the four-wave cycle "Ah" (Figure 26-2 and Table 26-1).

DOUBLE-WAVE ARITHMETIC

Two of the cycles ("AhHi" and "AhIe") have final points higher than the last point in the "Ah" cycle. The other two cycles ("AhHh"

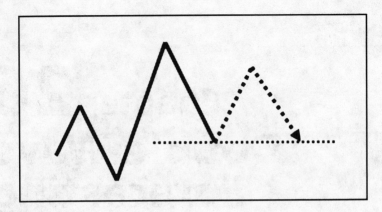

Figure 26-1   Double-Wave Extrapolation.

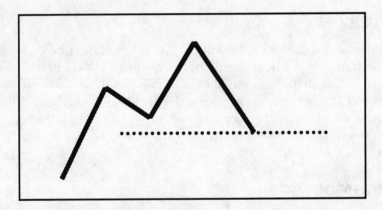

Figure 26-2   Four-Wave "Ah" Cycle.

Table 26-1   Raw Frequencies for "Ah" Cycle

Cycle ID	Frequency
AHHH	41
AHHI	203
AHIA	428
AHIE	340

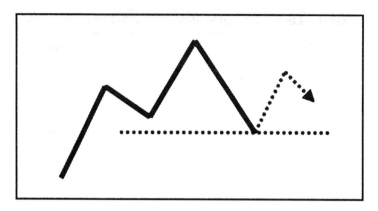

Figure 26-3   Double-Wave Forecast for "Ah" Cycle.

and "AhIa") have final points lower than the last point in the "Ah" cycle. Thus

Higher than last point $= 100 \times (203 + 340)/(41 + 203 + 428 + 340)$

Higher than last point $= 53.7$ percent

There is a 54 percent likelihood that an "Ah" cycle will be followed by two waves whose final price will be higher than the final price in the "Ah" cycle (Figure 26-3).

RESULTS (Table 26-2)

Unfortunately, the percentages of likelihood for price advances or price declines are insufficient in themselves to warrant any market entry orders because they do not deviate significantly from the 50 percent median. Nonetheless, this type of information may be useful when combined with other indicators. Interesting to note is that the height of the vertex between the fifth and sixth waves has an entirely neutral effect in this type of analysis.

Table 26-2   Double-Wave Forecast Percentages

Cycle ID	Higher	Lower
Ah	53.7	46.3
Ai	51.9	48.1
Ea	46.2	53.8
Ee	52.0	48.0
Hh	49.0	51.0
Hi	53.0	47.0
Ia	50.3	49.7
Ie	55.4	44.6

PART 10
Advanced Topics

Chapter **27**
Data Operations

TICK DATA

In order to compile an analytical study of this depth, it was necessary to acquire massive amounts of raw historical quotes. For these efforts, we wish to express our appreciation to Disk Trading, Ltd. (www.disktrading.com) for their extensive and well-organized archive of historical currency prices (both spot and futures) dating back to the early 1970s.

Forex data can be packaged either as streaming data or as interval data. Streaming data consist of every single price change as it occurs regardless of the time lapse between ticks. This creates huge amounts of data. For example, all the tick quotes for the EURUSD currency pair from January 1, 2005, to December 31, 2005, provide the statistical sample for numerous analyses in this book with a sample size of 7,974,098 prices.

Streaming data use the comma-delimited field conventions shown in Table 27-1 for tick data.

Data are shipped on compact disks and DVDs because the sheer volume of data is too large to download at current modem speeds. Comma-separated values (CSV) files must be unzipped and then read as flat ASCII files.

Table 27-1   EURUSD Streaming Tick Data

Date	Time	Price
2/3/2006	0830	1.2062
2/3/2006	0830	1.2064
2/3/2006	0830	1.2070
2/3/2006	0830	1.2066
2/3/2006	0830	1.2066
2/3/2006	0830	1.2087
2/3/2006	0830	1.2097
2/3/2006	0830	1.2101
2/3/2006	0830	1.2101
2/3/2006	0830	1.2099
2/3/2006	0830	1.2102
2/3/2006	0830	1.2102
2/3/2006	0830	1.2101
2/3/2006	0830	1.2105
2/3/2006	0830	1.2102

INTERVAL DATA

Interval data, on the other hand, are compiled from the streaming data by coercing them into the standard open, high, low, close (OHLC) format for equal-interval time periods. Disk Trading, Ltd., packages these types of data as 1-, 5-, 10-, and 30-minute, hourly, and daily data.

Interval data are stored in the convention shown in Table 27-2 (1-minute interval example).

Dates are always expressed using the standard convention MM/DD/YYYY, whereas the time field uses a four-digit integer to represent the 24-hour convention (i.e., 2030 = 8:30 p.m.).

Owing to the lack of centralization, Forex currency data do not have volume and open-interest fields as in commodity futures quotes. The last two fields above are upticks and downticks. These two fields can be used to calculate two indicators specific to currency trading, the *activity oscillator* and the *direction oscillator*.

UNRAVELING INTERVAL DATA

Most currency data vendors provide historical quote data in many different time intervals. Most typical are streaming ticks (closes

Table 27-2   EURUSD 1-Minute Interval Data

Date	Time	Open	High	Low	Close	Upticks	Downticks
1/6/2006	0830	1.2095	1.2098	1.2092	1.2094	110	120
1/6/2006	0831	1.2094	1.2142	1.2094	1.2123	225	228
1/6/2006	0832	1.2131	1.2134	1.2123	1.2124	260	311
1/6/2006	0833	1.2123	1.2132	1.2118	1.2125	274	284
1/6/2006	0834	1.2124	1.2129	1.2112	1.2115	246	280
1/6/2006	0835	1.2108	1.2128	1.2108	1.2123	264	267
1/6/2006	0836	1.2123	1.2124	1.2096	1.2098	229	263
1/6/2006	0837	1.2098	1.2110	1.2087	1.2095	288	240
1/6/2006	0838	1.2094	1.2112	1.2090	1.2112	228	250
1/6/2006	0839	1.2112	1.2119	1.2105	1.2112	215	203
1/6/2006	0840	1.2112	1.2119	1.2109	1.2112	171	167
1/6/2006	0841	1.2116	1.2117	1.2108	1.2113	182	232
1/6/2006	0842	1.2111	1.2124	1.2109	1.2123	216	224
1/6/2006	0843	1.2118	1.2122	1.2102	1.2114	192	179
1/6/2006	0844	1.2114	1.2117	1.2109	1.2114	126	128
1/6/2006	0845	1.2112	1.2116	1.2108	1.2113	145	165

only), 1-minute OHLC, 10-minute OHLC, 30-minute OHLC, hourly OHLC, and daily OHLC. However, most traders rarely have the need or the patience to deal directly with tick data (except during live trading sessions) because of their pure bulk and storage overhead. Critical analysts and statisticians do this job for the average trader.

When dealing with swing reversal algorithms, tick data may seem superfluous because the analyst is trying to filter out minor fluctuations anyway. Thus equispaced interval data are almost always employed.

All OHLC interval data have an intrinsic flaw by the mere fact that it is unknown which extreme occurred first, the high or the low. In our algorithms that convert raw data to both swing data and P&F data, we found it necessary to interject a preliminary process before actually filtering out fluctuations of a specified magnitude (i.e., lack of magnitude).

This process "unravels" the four OHLC quotes into four consecutive "closes" as it were, thus creating a stream of univariate data ideal for the swing reversal algorithm (also four times the size of the input data). Obviously, the opening and closing quotes pose no problem with regard to temporal order. The following rules determine which extreme occurred first:

Case 1: The open is closer to the high than the close (Figure 27-1).

Case 2: The open is closer to the low than the close (Figure 27-2).

Case 3: The open equals the close, and the open is closer to the high than the low (Figure 27-3).

Case 4: The open equals the close, and the open is closer to the low than the high (Figure 27-4).

Case 5: This is the unusually rare instance where the open equals the close, and both are equidistant from the extremes (Figure 27-5).

Rather than opt for a random determination of the high-low order, we decided to check the previous bar for any pertinent information and found two solutions (Figure 27-6).

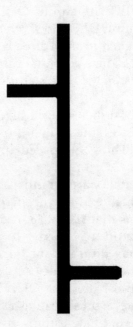

Figure 27-1   Order = O → H → L → C.

Figure 27-2 Order = O → L → H → C.

Figure 27-3 Order = O → H → L → C.

Figure 27-4   Order = O → L → H → C.

Figure 27-5   Open = Close.

Figure 27-6 Two Cases.

The two new rules for these conditions are

Case 5A: If the previous close is less than the current open (the left diagram), then the direction is upward. Therefore,

$$\text{Order} = O \rightarrow H \rightarrow L \rightarrow C$$

Case 5B: If the previous close is greater than the current open (the right diagram), then the direction is downward. Therefore,

$$\text{Order} = O \rightarrow L \rightarrow H \rightarrow C$$

Unfortunately, there remains one final case:

Case 5C: If the previous close equals the current open, then it is time to generate an equal-distribution random number (Figure 27-7).

We searched our 7 million + EURUSD 2005 database and found several instances of this condition. Fortunately, in every case the high equaled the low. Thus this occurs during periods of low activity and lateral congestion. We therefore feel justified in our very limited use of random numbers in a science where deterministic numbers are treasured.

As a matter of curiosity, currency traders may be interested to know just how many ticks can occur within a single minute

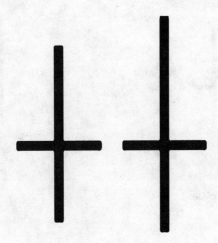

Figure 27-7   Order = O → ? → ? → C.

because this quantity less four quotes is being discarded by the "intervalizing" process. We searched our historical and more recent files and isolated the following:

Date: Wednesday, August 4, 2004
Time: 8:07 a.m. ET
Open: 1.2004
High: 1.2006
Low: 1.1970
Close: 1.1975
Upticks: 142
Downticks: 157

This amounts to 299 ticks in 1 minute with a range of 36 pips. Currency trading continues to grow at a phenomenal rate, so we expect this "record" to be broken in the very near future, quite possibly in one of the other major USD pairs or even a cross rate.

Chapter **28**
Swing Operations

FRACTAL LEVELS

In earlier chapters we mentioned using swing analysis at different fractal levels to determine the possible strength of a subsequent wave and its component waves. One method to perform this operation is to calculate swing data using two different minimum reversal amounts, say, a 5-pip reversal amount for the "child" fractal data and a 10-pip reversal amount for the "parent" swing data.

To perform this operation successfully, both sets of swing data must end on the same point, preferably the last known price in the raw data. Then, by using height-ratio wave comparisons at two levels, the trader can determine if the predicted waves will extend in the same price direction.

The disadvantage to this method is that prolonged experimentation may be required to discover a "perfect" child–parent fractal relationship. As markets become more volatile, higher reversal amounts may be required to filter out undesired white noise. As markets lose volatility, lower reversal amounts may be preferable. Also, there is the possibility that the difference in the two reversal amounts may be set too high. This will cause the fractal relationship to jump from a child–parent relationship to a child–grandparent relationship. An alternative method that progresses through each fractal level one at a time is given below.

PIVOT CHARTS

The *pivot chart* is a subset of the swing reversal chart that uses the bare minimum criteria as the parameters of the reversal algorithm. That is, the reversal increment is set to the minimum legal price fluctuation in the time series, and the number of reversal units is set to one. Paradoxically, this chart does not filter any reversals in price. The reason for this will become apparent shortly.

The pivot chart does, however, have the advantage of merging a multipoint trend into a single diagonal line. It also filters out horizontal price movements. Another advantage is that a pivot can be constructed easily by hand without the use of a software utility. All continuous upward movements resolve to the diagonal line, as do all continuous downward movements. There is no need to calculate a minimum reversal amount with each new price. The pivot chart is the only swing chart that can never have a child fractal chart. In other words, it is the lowest common denominator of all swing charts (Figure 28-1).

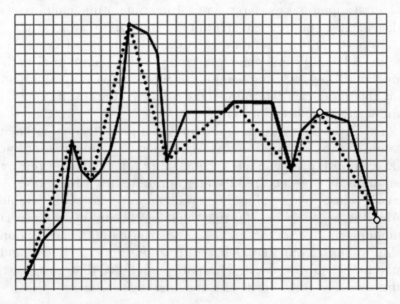

Figure 28-1 Pivot Chart.

We note in Figure 28-1 that no reversal is filtered out. A standard swing reversal chart of the same raw data (the solid curve) using a 15-pip reversal amount would generate only two diagonals, one bull wave followed by one bear wave.

CHANNEL LINES

The classification of the basic three-wave cycles discussed earlier will employ a rigid methodology that prevents any ambiguity: *channeling*. This is a purely mathematical process and has nothing to do with excursions into the supernatural.

All three-wave cycles always can be inscribed inside a channel quadrangle or triangle using the coordinate system shown in Table 28-1 (see Figure 28-2).

The upper boundary of the channel polygon (either a triangle or a parallelogram) passes through the two points $x2$, $y2$ and $x4$, $y4$, whereas the lower boundary of the channel shape passes through the two points $x1$, $y1$ and $x3$, $y3$, as depicted in Figure 28-3.

The criteria for classifying any three-wave cycle are derived from the *slopes* of its two identifying channel lines. In Figure 28-2, both slopes are positive, or travel from the lower left to the upper right of the diagram (the standard bull impulse cycle described earlier). The slope property of either channel line may have one of three mathematical attributes: *positive, negative,* or *zero*. These equate to upward, downward, and horizontal price movements.

The nine basic bull cycles with channel lines are shown in Figure 28-4.

Concerning the naming convention for triangles, the modifier *contracting* signifies that the channel lines converge on the right

Table 28-1 Cycle Coordinate System

Wave No.	Starting Point	Ending Point
1	$x1, y1$	$x2, y2$
2	$x2, y2$	$x3, y3$
3	$x3, y3$	$x4, y4$

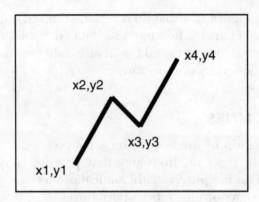

Figure 28-2   Impulse Cycle with Coordinates.

side of the cycle. Conversely, *expanding* indicates that the channel lines converge on the left of the cycle.

COLLAPSING CYCLES

The pivot chart in Figure 28-1 facilitates a very simple and direct approach to determining the parent fractal level of any swing data, which we refer to as *cycle collapsing*. To collapse any of the

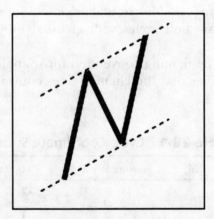

Figure 28-3   Three-Wave Impulse Cycle with Channel Lines.

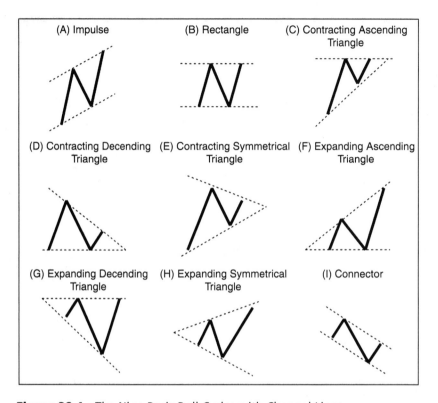

Figure 28-4 The Nine Basic Bull Cycles with Channel Lines.

three-wave bull cycles shown in Figure 28-4 into a single wave, the following two rules must be observed:

1. Using the coordinate system in Table 28-1, the starting point $y1$ must be lower than or equal to $y3$.
2. The ending point $y4$ must be greater than or equal to point $y2$.

If both conditions are satisfied, then the collapsing method is purely mechanical: Extend a straight line from the cycle starting coordinates $x1$, $y1$ to the cycle end point $x4$, $y4$. Examples are shown in Figure 28-5.

The four examples in this figure are, in fact, the only bull cycles that can be collapsed into a single wave in one operation. The

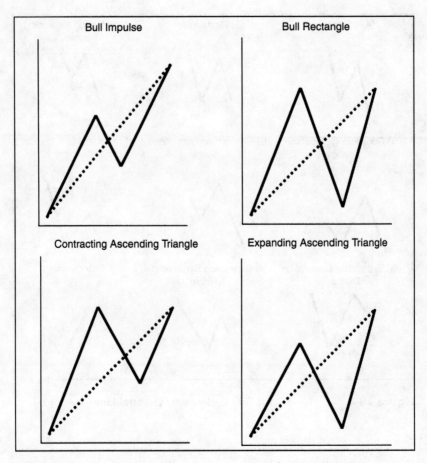

Figure 28-5 Collapsing Bull Cycles.

remaining five bull cycles (contracting descending triangle, contracting symmetrical triangle, expanding descending triangle, expanding symmetrical triangle, and the connector cycle) all violate one of the preceding rules (the bull connector cycle violates both rules).

Surprisingly, though, a second pass through the collapsed data will again collapse several three-wave cycles into a single wave. No more than two passes through the data are required to convert a set of swing data to its parent fractal data.

COLLAPSING MODES

There are two "modes" by which cycles may be collapsed: (1) single three-wave cycle collapsing and (2) continuous multiwave cycle collapsing.

Only one cycle at a time is converted when using the single three-wave cycle collapsing mode. On the other hand, the multiwave cycle collapsing mode will collapse any number of cycles until a noncollapsible cycle is encountered (Figure 28-6).

The leftmost cycle in this figure is a seven-wave bull impulse cycle without any collapsing. The center cycle is the result of single three-wave cycle collapsing. Note that the original cycle, designated "AiAiA," has been reduced to an "Ai" cycle.

We see that the rightmost "AiAiA" cycle has been converted to a single bull wave using continuous multiwave cycle collapsing. Extended impulse cycles always will reduce to a single diagonal regardless of the number of waves in the cycle.

Figures 28-7 and 28-8 present real-world examples of the different collapsing modes for the same data.

Single three-wave cycle collapsing produced a total of 39 waves, whereas continuous multiwave cycle collapsing reduced this amount to 13 diagonals.

Figure 28-6 Collapsing Modes.

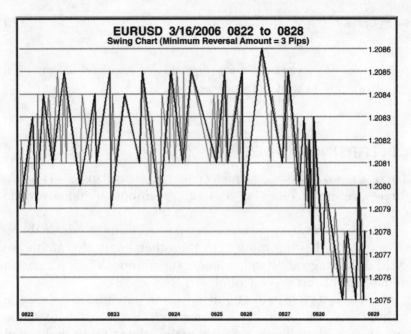

Figure 28-7   Single Three-Wave Cycle Collapsing.

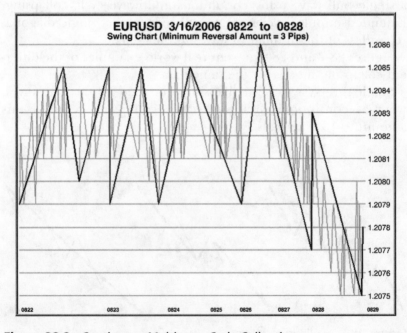

Figure 28-8   Continuous Multiwave Cycle Collapsing.

Chapter **29**
Practical Studies

OVERVIEW

Below are examples of how different minimum reversal amounts emphasize peaks and valleys under various market environments. Three dates were selected (01/06/2006, 02/03/2006, and 03/16/2006) on the basis of the sharp price spikes caused by news announcements from a variety of regulatory agencies. In all cases, price surges over 25 pips occurred in a single minute.

Each study has four 1-minute open, high, low, close (OHLC) charts overlaid with a swing reversal chart. Reversal amounts are 5, 10, 15, and 20 pips.

STUDY NO. 1—JANUARY 6, 2006
(Figures 29-1 through 29-4)

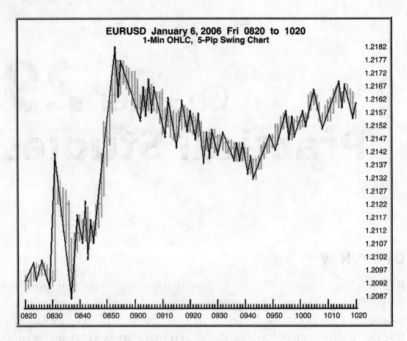

Figure 29-1   EURUSD 01/06/2006 5-Pip Reversal Amount.

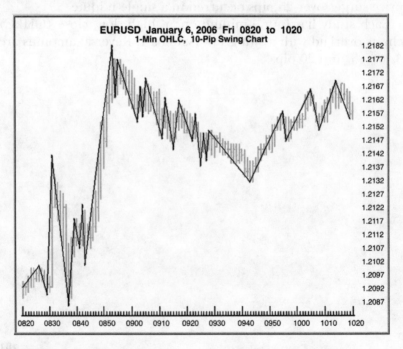

Figure 29-2   EURUSD 01/06/2006 10-Pip Reversal Amount.

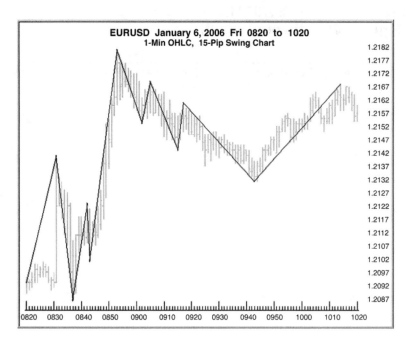

Figure 29-3 EURUSD 01/06/2006 15-Pip Reversal Amount.

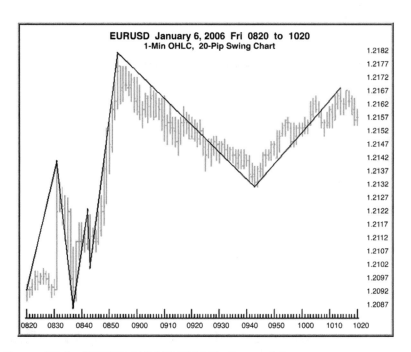

Figure 29-4 EURUSD 01/06/2006 20-Pip Reversal Amount.

STUDY NO. 2—FEBRUARY 3, 2006
(Figures 29-5 through 29-8)

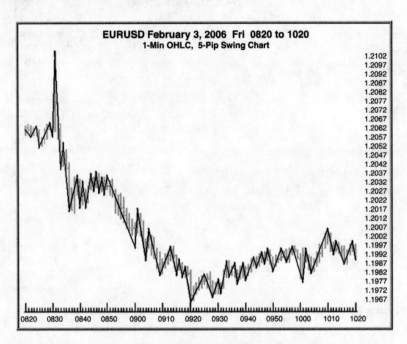

Figure 29-5   EURUSD 02/03/2006 5-Pip Reversal Amount.

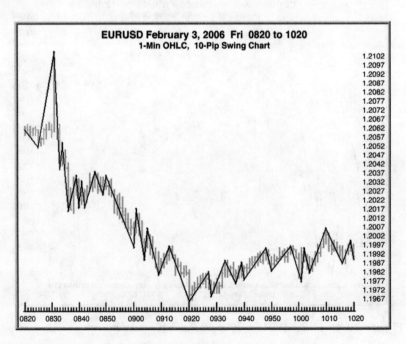

Figure 29-6   EURUSD 02/03/2006 10-Pip Reversal Amount.

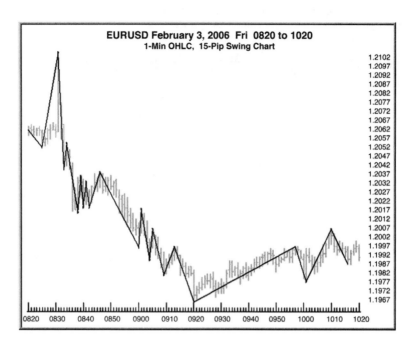

Figure 29-7 EURUSD 02/03/2006 15-Pip Reversal Amount.

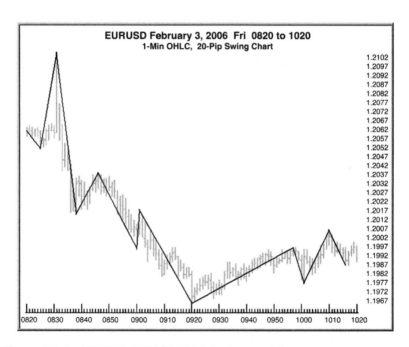

Figure 29-8 EURUSD 02/03/2006 20-Pip Reversal Amount.

STUDY NO. 3—MARCH 16, 2006
(Figures 29-9 through 29-12)

Figure 29-9 EURUSD 02/16/2006 5-Pip Reversal Amount.

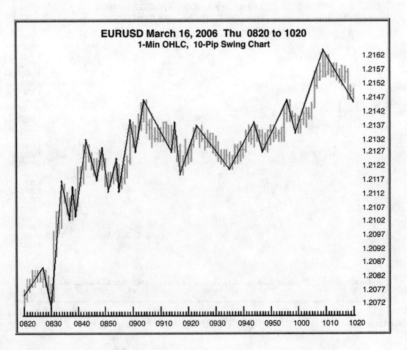

Figure 29-10 EURUSD 03/16/2006 10-Pip Reversal Amount.

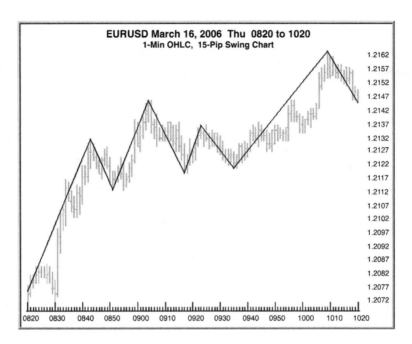

Figure 29-11 EURUSD 03/16/2006 15-Pip Reversal Amount.

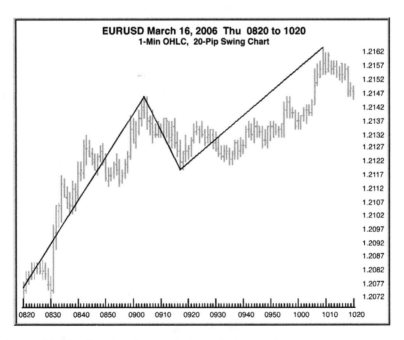

Figure 29-12 EURUSD 03/16/2006 20-Pip Reversal Amount.

SUMMARY

Calculating the number of swings that each reversal amount generates can be very useful when trying to determine the reversal amount for the next higher fractal level (Table 29-1). Flip books of fractal levels might be handy is this case.

Again, we will mention that swing data are bivariate in nature, that is, one price and one corresponding time index. In the charts shown in this chapter we see numerous instances where the slopes of the diagonal waves vary radically from just over a 0-degree horizontal line to an almost 90-degree incline. Generally speaking, the greater the absolute magnitude of the slope, the greater is the volume of trading.

If the cycle collapsing method were used to locate the next higher fractal level, the number of swings would be reduced by approximately three.

At this point, traders should have plenty of ammunition for applying wave theory to daily currency analysis. Granted, the majority of the tables in this book refer to the EURUSD currency pair, but with only minor modifications, they can be applied to the other major currency pairs as well.

Table 29-1   Reversal Amounts versus Number of Swings

Rev Amt	1/6/2006	2/3/2006	3/16/2006
5 Pips	57 Swings	59 Swings	58 Swings
10 Pips	32 Swings	35 Swings	26 Swings
15 Pips	11 Swings	22 Swings	8 Swings
20 Pips	7 Swings	11 Swings	3 Swings

Appendices

Appendix A: ISO Currencies Pairs

This is a list of global currencies and the three-character currency codes that we generally are used to represent them. Often, but not always, this code is the same as the ISO 4217 Standard. [The International Organization for Standardization (ISO) is a worldwide federation of national standards.]

In most cases, the currency code is composed of the country's two-character Internet country code plus an extra character to denote the currency unit. For example, the code for Canadian dollars is simply Canada's two-character Internet country code (CA) plus a one-character currency designator (D).

We have endeavored to list the codes that, in our experience, are actually in general industry use to represent the currencies. Currency names are given in the plural form. This list does not contain obsolete Euro-zone currencies.

Table A-1 World Currencies

Symbol	Region	Currency name
AED	United Arab Emirates	Dirhams
AFA	Afghanistan	Afghanis
ALL	Albania	Leke
AMD	Armenia	Drams
ANG	Netherlands Antilles	Guilders
AOA	Angola	Kwanza
ARS	Argentina	Pesos
AUD	Australia	Dollars
AWG	Aruba	Guilders
AZM	Azerbaijan	Manats
BAM	Bosnia, Herzegovina	Convertible marka
BBD	Barbados	Dollars
BDT	Bangladesh	Taka
BGN	Bulgaria	Leva
BHD	Bahrain	Dinars
BIF	Burundi	Francs
BMD	Bermuda	Dollars
BND	Brunei Darussalam	Dollars
BOB	Bolivia	Bolivianos
BRL	Brazil	Brazil real
BSD	Bahamas	Dollars
BTN	Bhutan	Ngultrum
BWP	Botswana	Pulas
BYR	Belarus	Rubles
BZD	Belize	Dollars
CAD	Canada	Dollars
CDF	Congo/Kinshasa	Congolese francs
CHF	Switzerland	Francs
CLP	Chile	Pesos
CNY	China	Renminbi
COP	Colombia	Pesos
CRC	Costa Rica	Colones
CUP	Cuba	Pesos
CVE	Cape Verde	Escudos
CYP	Cyprus	Pounds
CZK	Czech Republic	Koruny
DJF	Djibouti	Francs
DKK	Denmark	Kroner
DOP	Dominican Republic	Pesos
DZD	Algeria	Algeria dinars
EEK	Estonia	Krooni
EGP	Egypt	Pounds
ERN	Eritrea	Nakfa
ETB	Ethiopia	Birr
EUR	Euro member countries	Euro

(*Continued*)

Table A-1 (*Continued*)

Symbol	Region	Currency name
FJD	Fiji	Dollars
FKP	Falkland Islands	Pounds
GBP	United Kingdom	Pounds
GEL	Georgia	Lari
GGP	Guernsey	Pounds
GHC	Ghana	Cedis
GIP	Gibraltar	Pounds
GMD	Gambia	Dalasi
GNF	Guinea	Francs
GTQ	Guatemala	Quetzales
GYD	Guyana	Dollars
HKD	Hong Kong	Dollars
HNL	Honduras	Lempiras
HRK	Croatia	Kuna
HTG	Haiti	Gourdes
HUF	Hungary	Forint
IDR	Indonesia	Rupiahs
ILS	Israel	New shekels
IMP	Isle of Man	Pounds
INR	India	Rupees
IQD	Iraq	Dinars
IRR	Iran	Rials
ISK	Iceland	Kronur
JEP	Jersey	Pounds
JMD	Jamaica	Dollars
JOD	Jordan	Dinars
JPY	Japan	Yen
KES	Kenya	Shillings
KGS	Kyrgyzstan	Soms
KHR	Cambodia	Riels
KMF	Comoros	Francs
KPW	Korea (North)	Won
KRW	Korea (South)	Won
KWD	Kuwait	Dinars
KYD	Cayman Islands	Dollars
KZT	Kazakstan	Tenge
LAK	Laos	Kips
LBP	Lebanon	Pounds
LKR	Sri Lanka	Rupees
LRD	Liberia	Dollars
LSL	Lesotho	Maloti
LTL	Lithuania	Litai
LVL	Latvia	Lati
LYD	Libya	Dinars
MAD	Morocco	Dirhams

(*Continued*)

Table A-1 (*Continued*)

Symbol	Region	Currency name
MDL	Moldova	Lei
MGA	Madagascar	Ariary
MKD	Macedonia	Denars
MMK	Myanmar (Burma)	Kyats
MNT	Mongolia	Tugriks
MOP	Macau	Patacas
MRO	Mauritania	Ouguiyas
MTL	Malta	Liri
MUR	Mauritius	Rupees
MVR	Maldives	Rufiyaa
MWK	Malawi	Kwachas
MXN	Mexico	Pesos
MYR	Malaysia	Ringgits
MZM	Mozambique	Meticais
NAD	Namibia	Dollars
NGN	Nigeria	Nairas
NIO	Nicaragua	Gold cordobas
NOK	Norway	Krone
NPR	Nepal	Nepal rupees
NZD	New Zealand	Dollars
OMR	Oman	Rials
PAB	Panama	Balboa
PEN	Peru	Nuevos soles
PGK	Papua New Guinea	Kina
PHP	Philippines	Pesos
PKR	Pakistan	Rupees
PLN	Poland	Zlotych
PYG	Paraguay	Guarani
QAR	Qatar	Rials
ROL	Romania	Lei
RUR	Russia	Rubles
RWF	Rwanda	Rwanda francs
SAR	Saudi Arabia	Riyals
SBD	Solomon Islands	Dollars
SCR	Seychelles	Rupees
SDD	Sudan	Dinars
SEK	Sweden	Kronor
SGD	Singapore	Dollars
SHP	Saint Helena	Pounds
SIT	Slovenia	Tolars
SKK	Slovakia	Koruny
SLL	Sierra Leone	Leones
SOS	Somalia	Shillings
SPL	Seborga	Luigini
SRG	Suriname	Guilders

(*Continued*)

Table A-1 (Continued)

Symbol	Region	Currency name
STD	São Tome, Principe	Dobras
SVC	El Salvador	Colones
SYP	Syria	Pounds
SZL	Swaziland	Emalangeni
THB	Thailand	Baht
TJS	Tajikistan	Somoni
TMM	Turkmenistan	Manats
TND	Tunisia	Dinars
TOP	Tonga	Pa'anga
TRL	Turkey	Liras
TTD	Trinidad, Tobago	Dollars
TVD	Tuvalu	Tuvalu dollars
TWD	Taiwan	New dollars
TZS	Tanzania	Shillings
UAH	Ukraine	Hryvnia
UGX	Uganda	Shillings
USD	United States of America	Dollars
UYU	Uruguay	Pesos
UZS	Uzbekistan	Sums
VEB	Venezuela	Bolivares
VND	Viet Nam	Dong
VUV	Vanuatu	Vatu
WST	Samoa	Tala
XAF	Communauté Financière Africaine	Francs
XAG	Silver	Ounces
XAU	Gold	Ounces
XCD	East Caribbean	Dollars
XDR	International Monetary Fund	Special drawing rights
XOF	Communauté Financière Africaine	Francs
XPD	Palladium	Ounces
XPF	Comptoirs Français du Pacifique	Francs
XPT	Platinum	Ounces
YER	Yemen	Rials
YUM	Yugoslavia	New dinars
ZAR	South Africa	Rand
ZMK	Zambia	Kwacha
ZWD	Zimbabwe	Zimbabwe dollars

Appendix B: Exchange Rates

Table B-1 shows the international foreign exchange rates on 04/21/2006 compared with the USD.

Table B-1   Exchange Rates

Currency	Units/USD	USD/Units
Algerian dinar	0.01379	72.52500
Argentine peso	0.32701	3.05800
Australian dollar	0.74420	1.34373
Baharaini dinar	2.65266	0.37698
Bolivian boliviano	0.12508	7.99500
Brazilian real	0.47279	2.11510
British pound	1.78280	0.56092
Botswana pula	0.18714	5.34360
Canadian dollar	0.87827	1.13860
Chilean peso	0.00193	517.54999
Chinese yuan	0.12477	8.01450
Columbian peso	0.00043	2,337.00004
Cypriot pound	2.14777	0.46560
Czech koruna	0.04359	22.94200
Danish krone	0.16547	6.04350
Ecuador sucre	0.00004	25,000.00063
Euro	1.23450	0.81005
Ghanaian cedi	0.00011	9,106.99988

(*Continued*)

Table B-1 (*Continued*)

Currency	Units/USD	USD/Units
Guatemalan quetzal	0.13201	7.57500
Hong Kong dollar	0.12897	7.75400
Hungarian forint	0.00467	213.96001
Israeli shekel	0.22015	4.54230
Indian rupee	0.02216	45.13500
Indonesian rupiah	0.00011	8,882.99974
Japanese yen	0.00855	116.93001
Jordanian dinar	1.41143	0.70850
Kenyan shilling	0.01404	71.22000
Kuwaiti dinar	3.42407	0.29205
Malaysian ringgit	0.27319	3.66050
Mexican peso	0.09016	11.09120
Moroccan dirham	0.11191	8.93550
Namibian dollar	0.16587	6.02900
New Zealand dollar	0.63330	1.57903
Norwegian krone	0.15748	6.35000
Omani rial	2.59774	0.38495
Pakistan rupee	0.01668	59.97000
Peruvian nuevo sol	0.30233	3.30770
Qatari rial	0.27467	3.64070
Russian ruble	0.03639	27.48000
Saudi riyal	0.26663	3.75050
Singapore dollar	0.62661	1.59590
South African rand	0.16707	5.98550
South Korean won	0.00106	948.00005
Swedish krona	0.13248	7.54860
Swiss franc	0.78475	1.27430
Taiwan dollar	0.03098	32.27500
Tanzanian shilling	0.00083	1,211.99996
Thai baht	0.02645	37.81000
Tunisian dinar	0.74738	1.33800
Turkish lira	0.75683	1.32130
UAR Emirati dirham	0.27228	3.67270
U.S. dollar	1.00000	1.00000
Venezualan bolivar	0.00047	2,144.00005
Vietnamese dong	0.00006	15,924.99916
Zimbabwe dollar	0.00001	99,202.00100

It is interesting to note that as of the date above, only six world currencies have a parity rate with the USD greater than 1.0000: Kuwaiti dinar (3.42407), Baharaini dinar (2.65266), Omani rial (2.59774), Cypriot pound (2.14777), British pound (1.78280), and the Euro (1.23450). Coincidentally, at the bottom of the list, both alphabetically and parity-wise, is the Zimbabwe dollar, which requires over 99,000 to equal 1 USD.

Additional information on current exchange rates can be found at http://moneycentral.msn.com/investor/market/rates.asp.

Appendix C: Global Banking Hours

Price fluctuations in the spot currency markets are essentially news-driven. Or more accurately, it is the human reaction to news-driven events that makes trading possible and profitable. How traders interpret these news events determines which direction the market will travel. As in all financial markets, the Forex market also has its share of contrarians who keep runaway breakouts in check while supplying additional volatility to the overall situation.

Despite all the fundamental and technical influences on the Forex, one major constant in determining periods of high volatility is the hours of operation for the central banks of each major currency country.

The following table emphasizes the importance of the effect of time of day on Forex market activity and volatility based on hours of operation around the globe. Because banking hours vary from country to country, we have arbitrarily set hours of operation from 9:00 a.m. to 5:00 p.m. for consistency. The top row is expressed as Central European Time (Greenwich Mean Time + 1 hour), which aligns with the Central Bank of Europe in Frankfurt, the most prestigious central bank in the European Monetary Union.

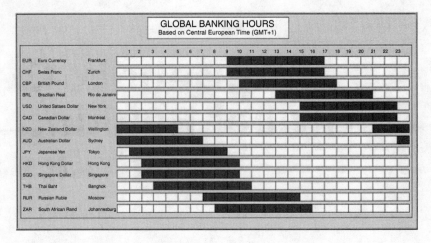

Figure C-1 Global Banking Hours.

This table allows traders to view overlapping time periods when central banks for different currencies are operating and thus guarantees a certain degree of mutual activity.

For example, when banks open in New York City at 9:00 a.m. EST, the Frankfurt bank already has been operating for six hours. Thus there is a two-hour overlap of trading in the EURUSD currency pair on both sides of the Atlantic Ocean (9:00 to 11:00 a.m. EST). This can be readily recognized in the time-of-day activity chart for the EURUSD pair.

If we are interested in initiating a trade in the EURHKD cross-rate pair, we note that there is a one-hour overlap in banking operations between central Europe and Hong Kong that occurs between 9:00 and 10:00 a.m. in Frankfurt (or 3:00 to 4:00 a.m. in New York).

Dedicated currency traders may have to adjust their sleeping schedules to take advantage of increased activity and volatility when trading non-USD cross-rate currency pairs.

Appendix D: Basic Three-Wave Cycles

The nine three-wave bull cycles with channel lines are as shown in Figure D-1.

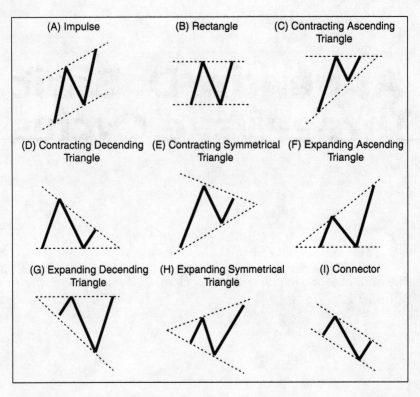

Figure D-1   Basic Three-Wave Cycles.

Appendix E: Resources

PERIODICALS

Active Trader (TechInfo, Inc.): www.activetradermag.com.
Futures (Futures Magazine, Inc.): www.futuresmag.com.
Currency Trader: www.currencytradermag.com.
EForex: www.eforex.net.
Euromoney: www.euromoney.com.
FX&MM: www.russellpublishing.com/FX&MM/index.html.
FX Week: www.fxweek.com.
Technical Analysis of Stocks & Commodities: www.traders.com.
Traders Journal: www.traders-journal.com.

BOOKS

Archer, Michael, and Bickford James, *Getting Started in Currency Trading* (New York: Wiley, 2004).

DraKoln, Noble, *Forex for Small Speculators* (New York: Enlightened, 2004).

Henderson, Callum, *Currency Strategy* (New York: Wiley, 2002).

Horner, Raghee, *Forex Trading for Maximum Profit* (New York: Wiley, 2005).

Klopfenstein, Gary, *Trading Currency Cross Rates* (New York: Wiley, 1993).

Lien, Kathy, *Day Trading the Currency Market* (New York: Wiley, 2004).

Louw, G. N., *Begin Forex* (New York: FXTrader, 2003).

Luca, Cornelius, *Technical Analysis Applications in the Global Currency Markets* (Englewood Cliffs, NJ: Prentice-Hall, 2000).

Luca, Cornelius, *Trading in the Global Currency Markets* (Englewood Cliffs, NJ: Prentice-Hall, 2000).

Murphy, John, *Intermarket Financial Analysis* (New York: Wiley, 2000).

Murphy, John, *Technical Analysis of the Financial Markets* (Englewood Cliffs, NJ: Prentice-Hall, 1999).

Reuters, Ltd., *An Introduction to Foreign Exchange and Money Markets* (New York: Reuters Financial Training, 1999).

Rosenstreich, Peter, *Forex Revolution* (Englewood Cliffs, NJ: Prentice-Hall, 2004).

Schlossberg, Boris, *Technical Analysis of the Currency Market* (New York: Wiley, 2006).

Shamah, Shani, *A Foreign Exchange Primer* (New York: Wiley, 2003).

Thousands of books have been written on the subject of technical analysis. Here are a few with possible topical interest to this volume:

Aby, Carroll D, Jr., *Point and Figure Charting* (New York: Traders Press, 1996).

Bigalow, Stephen, *Profitable Candlestick Trading* (New York: Wiley, 2002).

Bickford, James, *Chart Plotting Techniques for Technical Analysts* (Syzygy, 2002).

Bulkowski, Thomas, *Encyclopedia of Chart Patterns* (New York: Wiley, 2005).

Dorsey, Thomas, *Point and Figure Charting* (New York: Wiley, 1995).

Lindsay, Charles, *Trident: A Trading Strategy* (New York: Trident, 1976).

McGee, John, *Technical Analysis of Stock Trends* (New York: American Management Association, 2001).

Nison, Steve, *Japanese Candlestick Charting Techniques* (New York: Hall, 2001).

Nofri, Eugene, and Nofri-Steinberg, Jeanette, *Success in Commodities* (New York: Success, 1975).

Ross, Joe, *Trading by the Minute* (Joe Ross, 1991).

Zieg, Kermit, *Point and Figure* (Greenville, SC: Traders Press), 1997.
A fine resource is www.traderspress.com.

INTERNET

The amount of information now on the Internet about currency trading is enormous—a Google search finds over 2.2 million entries for "Forex"; inclusion herein does not represent an endorsement of any kind. We suggest beginning with one of the major Portals such as www.goforex.net.

ONLINE BROKERS AND DEALERS

www.abwatley.com/forex/
www.ac-markets.com/
www.admisi.com
www.advancedfinancialworldwideinc.com
www.akmos.com/
www.alphaonetrading.com
www.ancofutures.com
www.apexforex.com
www.alipes.net
www.arcadiavest.com
www.axistrader.com
www.cbfx.com
www.charterfx.com
www.choicefx.com
www.cmc-forex.com
www.cms-forex.com
www.coesfx.com
www.csfb.com
www.currencyconnect.net/
www.currencytradingusa.com
www.currencyuk.co.uk/
www.currenex.com
www.cytradefutures.com
www.dfgforex.com

www.directfx.com
www.dukascopy.com
www.eminilocal.com
www.enetspeculation.com/pub/en/defaut.asp
www.etradeprofessional.co.uk
www.fibo-forex.it
www.finanza.saav.biz
www.FlashForex.com
www.forex.com
www.forex.ukrsotsbank.com
www.forexcapital.com
www.forex-arabia.com
www.forex-day-trading.com
www.forexforyou.com
www.forex-mg.com
www.forex-millenium.com
www.forexsolutions.com
www.forextradingusa.com
www.forextradingdirect.com
www.forexsystembroker.com
www.fxadvantage.com
www.fxall.com
www.fxcm.com
www.fxdd.com
www.fxonline.co.jp
www.fxpremier.com
www.fxsol.com
www.fxtrader.net
www.fxtrading.com
www.gaincapital.com
www.gcitrading.com
www.gfsbroker.com
www.gftforex.com
www.ggmk.com
www.gnitouch.com
www.goldbergforex.com
www.guardianfx.com
www.hawaii4x.com
www.hotspotfx.com

www.ifxmarkets.com
www.interactivebrokers.com
www.interbankfx.com
www.invest2forex.com
www.kshitij.com/
www.mvpglobalforex.com
www.oio.com
www.pfgbest.com
www.powerforex.com
www.proedgefx.com
www.propfx.com
www.rcgtrader.com
www.realtimeforex.com
www.realtrade.lv
www.refcofx.com/
www.rjobrien.com
www.saxobank.com/
www.socofinance.com
www.sncinvestment.com
www.spencerfx.com
www.strategybroker.comhttp://www.strikefx.com
www.superfutures.com
www.swissnetbroker.com
www.synthesisbank.com
www.titanfingroup.com
www.tradeamerican.com
www.tradestation.com
www.x-trade.biz
www.zaner.com

Data

www.ozforex.tradesecuring.com/misc/ozchart.asp
www.csidata.com
www.forexcapital.com/database.htm
www.olsendata.com
www.disktrading.is99.com/disktrading
www.cqg.com/products/datafactory.cfm
www.datastream.com

www.tenfore.com
www.dukascopy.com
www.netdania.com
www.pctrader.com
www.csidata.com
www.ebs.com/products/market-data.asp
www.infotecnet.com
www.comstock-interactivedata.com/index.shtml

Charts

www.fxtrek.com
www.esignal.com
www.forex-markets.com/
www.forexcharts.com/
www.moneytec.com
www.global-view.com/beta
www.fxstreet.com
www.forexdirectory.net
www.forex-markets.com

Portals, Link Pages, and Forums

www.moneytec.com
www.goforex.com
www.forexsites.com
www.investorsresource.info
www.global-view.com/beta
www.fxstreet.com
www.forexdirectory.net
www.forexvision.com
www.currencypro.com
www.forexcentral.net
www.forexpoint.com
www.piptrader.com
www.forex-registry.com

Software Development

www.snapdragon.co.uk
www.fxpraxis.com

Performance Evaluation

www.parkerglobal.com
www.marhedge.com
www.barclaygrp.com

Professional and Regulatory

www.aima.org
www.cftc.gov
www.nfa.futures.org
www.mfainfo.org
www.fiafii.org

Index

About the Author

James Bickford began trading commodity futures in the early 1980s. Since 2001, he has focused his investment efforts solely on trading spot currency pairs via online Forex dealers. His academic background is in computer science, applied mathematics, and statistics. By profession, he has been a software engineer for nearly three decades. He has authored and coauthored several books on technical analysis and currency trading: *Chart Plotting Algorithms for Technical Analysts* (Syzygy Publishing, 2001), *Getting Started in Currency Trading* (Wiley, 2005), *Forex Chartist's Companion: A Visual Approach to Technical Analysis* (Wiley, 2006), and *Forex Trader's Companion: Focus on Major Currencies* (Wiley, 2007).